SUCCESS IS A TEAM EFFORT

No One Succeeds Alone

Compiled by Doug Smart

James &
Brookfield

J&B

Publishers

SUCCESS IS A TEAM EFFORT

Managing Editor: Gayle Smart
Editor: Sara Kahan
Proofing Editor: Laura Johnson
Book Designer: Paula Chance
Copyright ©2000

Disclaimer: This book is a compilation of ideas
from numerous experts who have each contributed a chapter.
As such, the views expressed in each chapter are those of the authors
and not necessarily the views of James & Brookfield Publishers.

For more information, contact:
James & Brookfield Publishers
P.O. Box 768024
Roswell, GA 30076
℃ 770-587-9784

Library of Congress Catalog Number 00-106610

ISBN: 0-9658893-7-8

10 9 8 7 6 5 4 3 2 1

CONTENTS

GREAT MANNERS MAKE FOR GREAT BUSINESS: ADDING POLISH TO PROFESSIONALISM

by Cecilia B. Grimes

In today's ever-demanding business arena, knowing all about your particular field of expertise is not the starting place — your manners are. When you bring your ideas to the meeting, your briefcase to the conference table, your proposal to the committee, your calculations to the board, you also bring the "essence of you"— and in a civilized world, that's your grasp of manners. How you project civility, consideration, and common courtesy impacts how your ideas are received. The concept is simple, straightforward, powerful, valuable, and true: *Great Manners Make for Great Business!*

Think of "polish" as the name we give to this valuable concept. We routinely use polish in other dimensions of our lives: we seek to add gloss and glimmer to our table settings, our Christmas packages, our holiday attire, our party decorations and invitations, our jewelry. We shine our shoes, we buff our fingernails, we wax our cars, we rub lemon oil on our furniture. Why not a healthy swipe of polish, applied purposefully and consistently, to ourselves as individuals?

Polishing the Professional Presence: Extending Manners to Business Cards

Let's begin with one small aspect of professional presence: the courteous and impressive ritual of a business card. Here's an easy opportunity for a professional to shine!

How do you carry your business cards? A plastic case will keep your cards clean and together, but what does a plastic carrying case project? How about loose cards, perhaps slipped in a suit pocket or a purse? In either of these scenarios, the cards are readily available, but the approach is not polished. Such cards would be easily tattered and soiled, and therefore unusable.

A first-class approach would be to transport your clean, crisp business cards in a small leather card case: neat, classy, professional. POLISHED!

Once you have secured the outward case for your business cards, turn your attention to the presentation of business cards. Keep your recipient in mind when you present your card. Always present a business card so that the writing faces the recipient. Another small consideration is for those who might be using reading glasses when they refer to your card. Request from the printer a font size for the primary contact number (the preferred number where you can most easily be reached) that is large enough to read without magnifying glasses. (Generally speaking, a font size 12 or larger works well.) It's the little things that make an impression.

When you are the recipient of a business card, you should also project polish. Pause long enough to look at the card. Show some interest in the information, whether clarifying an address or commenting on a logo or an unusual style. The exchange need not be a lengthy one, but as a courtesy give a bit of attention to some aspect of the card. Also be aware that in some cultures, it is especially important to extend courtesy not only to the individual who presents the card but also to the card itself. Receive a business card with a professional, rather than casual, approach, and conclude the exchange by placing the card in a front rather than a rear pocket. Such courtesies with a business card show great manners, and great manners make for great business.

Polishing the Professional Presence: Extending Manners to Handshakes and Introductions

Handshakes have been called the universal greeting, and as such deserve more attention than we often give them in our culture. There's more to a correct handshake than the grasping of another's hand. When the hand is offered, the thumb should be in an upright position, and as the hands connect, the web of each hand should touch. This correct positioning precludes a delicate "tips-of-the-fingers" approach, which is considered inappropriate in the business arena, and prevents the equally inappropriate harsh and painful squeezing of the lower fingers. Women and men should offer this professional handshake as evidence of their polished presence.

Equally important are introductions, that vehicle by which we come to know others and for others to know us. An outstretched hand poised for a handshake, the repeating of our name to another with a gracious greeting, and a smile are the three preliminaries for a self-directed introduction. This approach engenders goodwill and sets the stage for a gracious encounter. Those on the receiving end of such courtesies appreciate a name being offered forthrightly, as no one is immune to the dreaded memory lapse when it comes to names. Improve your ability to recall names by silently and swiftly repeating to yourself three or four times the name you have just heard in an introduction. In the ensuing conversation, address that person by name. Imprinting in your mind's eye will be taking place!

So often we become involved with the mechanics of an introduction that we actually let the name slip by. Establishing eye contact and getting ready for the handshake, important as they are, should not divert us from the most significant component of an introduction: hearing that name! Discipline yourself to listen carefully for the name being offered before initiating the handshake. We can't imprint in our mind's eye a name we have not truly heard. Always stand for handshakes and introductions. Standing conveys respect and establishes a professional presence.

Polishing the Professional Presence: Extending Manners to Mobile Phones

Telephones, Telephones, Telephones! Whether we're in the seminar room or a board meeting, walking the hallways of an airport, riding in our automobile, dining in a fine restaurant, playing a round of golf, attending a class, mingling at a cocktail party, or attending a concert or sports event, we're wired for constant and instant access. Think of the myriad opportunities to project a professional presence with mobile phones: They abound!

Begin with a conscientious, rather than territorial, regard for personal space. Just how much space belongs to any one person in a conference room or at a sports arena? And what does your use of that personal space radiate about the "essence of you"? Plenty!

Because personal space in such settings is fluid, it's easy to offend. Answering a loud ring and commencing an animated conversation without regard for the presence of others falls into the category of blatant rudeness. It's an invasion of shared space, it's disruptive, and it shows a lack of good manners.

The length of your involvement with any call and your voice level are also indicators of your manners. Keep any conversation brief and your voice tone low until you can discreetly withdraw from shared space. When you respond, alert the caller to your dilemma, politely excuse yourself to those around, and continue your conversation when you move to a less disruptive place. A true emergency aside, rarely is it appropriate to continue a conversation in such communal settings.

Within shared space, the first courtesy with a mobile phone is to turn the ringer as low as possible. Ideally, you should turn the ringer off and switch to the vibrating mode. You retain the ability to be reached, but you minimize disruption for others.

A quiet tone of voice removes the impression that your call is more important than the business at hand. It also removes the impression of self-promotion and self-importance. The rest of us don't want to hear the details of a disgruntled employee's most recent outburst back at the office, what time you're expected for supper, what groceries you need to purchase on your way home, or why your stockbroker doesn't recommend that stock purchase. We are, however, quite tolerant, even understanding, of your need to touch base with loved ones, check messages at the office, and make reservations for an important business luncheon. Just accomplish these tasks in your space and not ours!

Polishing your Professional Presence:
Extending Manners with Handwritten Notes

Few people take the time these days to hand-write notes, but the power to impress through such notes is difficult to overstate. Combine professionalism with polish, and accept this three-tier, time-honored approach to note-writing:

- It's important to write them.
- It's important to write them right.
- It's important to write them promptly.

First, make a decision that notes are important and that you will commit to writing them.

Continue to send "messages" by e-mail, but look for the opportunities in your life — both personal and professional — to send personally scripted notes. Think back to last week. How many people with whom you came into contact would have benefited from a personal note? How about the attentive server who was superb during your company's awards banquet, the thoughtful parking attendant who retrieved your umbrella, the dynamic speaker at Rotary who struck a chord with your sentiments, your favorite third-grade teacher who just retired? Find something noteworthy and you have the basis for a note. Write notes of congratulations, appreciation, gratitude, and condolence. Send them to friends, neighbors, family, wait staff, colleagues, and clients. Hand-write them and experience their power to spread good will and create joy!

Understand that the hallmark of a first-class note is one that the recipient will keep or share. (A generic note will never be kept — it'll always be tossed!) Begin with clean, crisp stationery and use black ink for a professional appearance. Observe margins — top, bottom, left and right. It may take a bit of planning, but writing that continues all the way to the edges robs the note of symmetry. Include a date in the top right side of the note and a salutation with a comma as the correct punctuation. The closing (which will line up exactly with the date) is also followed by a comma.

Project professionalism by focusing on the client or patron, rather than yourself. Start the note with you, rather than "I". (Remember: It's more about thee, than me!) Find another way to say "thank you" without using those words. Provide some personal recollection, some mutual frame of reference, some specific detail that lifts your writing, and thus your note, from the generic.

Here's how that might work in an incident with a parking attendant.

April 24, xxxx

Dear Paul,

 You made my day last evening when you returned the small black umbrella you found in the parking lot. At first glance it may appear to be just another black umbrella, but it was a gift from a favorite uncle and it is quite special. Imagine my distress when I first realized it was gone and then later the sense of relief and delight when you brought it over to the car with the keys. You came to my rescue, and I am most grateful!

Sincerely,
Michael Armstrong

The mechanics are correct, and four sentences later you have expressed true gratitude and put evidence of that in another hand. Note that the note focuses on Paul: Paul's conscientious retrieval of the umbrella, Paul's saving the day, Paul's rescue, Paul's turning an incident from distress to delight. The incident is rather small, perhaps insignificant to some, but think of the impression on the provider of the good deed. And one good deed deserves another!

The note moves beyond the generic because it contains specific details (rather than generalities), puts the "storyline" in some context to which both parties can relate, and is cordial and courteous in tone. Its other big plus is that it actually became a written document which could be enjoyed and appreciated by the recipient. The more promptly a note is written, the more impressive the exchange will be. We all can plead busy schedules, but even the very busy find time to read, savor, and appreciate well-chosen words penned on crisp stationery! The process is easier if you keep close at hand a folder containing a good writing pen, your personal stationery, and a supply of interesting stamps.

Write one such note every week for a year and enjoy extending your manners through handwritten notes. It's true what the old proverb teaches, "The good you do will return to you."

Polishing the Professional Presence:
Extending Manners to Dining

So much of today's business takes place over a meal, whether an executive breakfast, a luncheon board meeting, or a business dinner. It is an established fact that most companies and corporations of the world are demanding a certain level of dining expertise. Often prospective employees are interviewed over a meal. Colleges and universities who are in the business of training the workforce are taking note that tomorrow's employers want polished individuals who understand this business dynamic: Great manners make for great business, and a great deal of business takes place while dining!

Dining at its finest may include sumptuous food, fine wines, heirloom china, sterling silverware, and sparkling crystal. The ritual may be shared with important clients and savvy colleagues, with family and friends. The conversation may be lively and stimulating, but the occasion will not be all that it should be if the diners do not bring a certain polish and finesse to the shared dining experience.

Co-existing between diners and a well-trained wait staff is a Silent Service Code that is characterized by reciprocity, grace, and good will. Knowledge of this code allows both diners and wait staff to participate in a shared process of mutual consideration. The desired outcome, a pleasant and pleasurable dining experience for all, is accomplished between diner and staff, working in concert. It is a matter of silent signals, and polished diners understand them.

Learn from this real-life lesson.

Once at a gathering of several hundred dinner guests in a large ballroom in Florida, I was seated next to a lovely woman who happened to be from my home state. We had pleasantly chatted through the first two courses of a multi-course meal, and then she asked a favor of me. Each evening at exactly nine o'clock, she returned to her hotel room for a telephone call about a family member who had become ill since her departure. The favor she required of me was to "tell" the server not to remove her plate of food as she would be returning shortly. Having made this request, she swiftly departed the company of those at our table and tossed her napkin onto the table to the left of her plate. Little did she know that the napkin toss contradicted her intentions to return.

Responding to her request, I reached over and pulled the corner of her napkin so that it dropped onto the seat of her chair. Moments later, the server passed by her chair. Trained to "read" this signal, he lifted the napkin from the seat, refolded it, vertically placed it across the back of the chair, and moved on.

Returning shortly, my dinner companion expressed gratitude for my assistance, "Thank you so much for *telling* the server not to take my plate. They took it away last night, and I wasn't finished!"

Of course, the food was removed the night before because that is the signal that she gave. Unaware of the silent service code, she had signaled closure to the meal by returning the napkin to the table to the left of the plate.

A napkin is correctly removed from the table when the meal begins and does not return to the table until the meal is completed. At formal occasions the host or hostess leads the way. A hostess will remove the napkin from the table and place it on her lap as a signal that the meal is to begin. When she lifts her fork, others should follow. All diners should wait for that moment when these silent signals are given and proceed likewise. Diners who are unaware of such protocols run the risk of commencing a meal before preliminaries such as grace, a toast to a guest of honor, or a "Bon appetit" greeting occur. The correct posture is to wait for the hostess's silent signal before sipping a bit of water, touching the plate, moving the silverware, or removing the napkin.

At larger banquet settings, it is a bit trickier if the setup is for large round tables and there is no designated hostess or host. If it is likely your table will fill quickly, then resist the temptation to begin without your dinner companions. It's a self-discipline that reaps great rewards in good will. Wait to begin, in consideration for others. Common courtesy and common sense, however, should rule the day, as it would be foolish to allow your food to cool for the sake of lagging companions.

Often during the course of a meal, a diner pauses or "rests." During these periods of time, there are important positions for the silverware that convey resting, and a polished diner and a well-trained wait staff observe them. Learn these positions and you won't have to deal with overzealous servers who appear eager to remove your plate at the first opportune moment.

The resting signals vary between the two major styles: American and Continental. Let's look at each. The American style of dining is used by those who dine primarily with one hand, switch the fork from one hand to the other after cutting food with the knife, and return the other hand to the lap. American-style diners signal resting by putting a few inches of space between the fork and knife as they rest on the plate. Imagine the plate as the face of a clock. In the American style, the fork "rests" at the 4:20 position on the plate and the knife rests diagonally across the top right side of the plate. Three or four inches of space separate the two utensils. The ends of the silverware usually extend about a half-inch over the edge of the plate. Diners who are engaged in conversation, who wish to sip a beverage, or who leave the table briefly will employ this aspect of the silent service code to convey "resting." By contrast, the Continental style of dining allows a diner to rest the forearms, just above the wrists, on the tabletop and retain, throughout the entire meal, the fork in the left hand and the knife in the right hand. The resting position for this style of dining is definitive: The knife is placed at 4:20, blade facing inward toward the diner, and the fork is placed at 8:10, tines down, across the knife.

At the meal's conclusion, a diner silently signals "I am finished" by placing the fork and knife side by side at the 4:20 position. The fork should be to the left of the knife. The "I am finished" signal is the same for both the American and the Continental styles of dining. (Even left-handed diners should observe this courtesy to the server, who will be removing the plate and silverware from the right.) Reciprocity and good will reign, and the signals are silent!

A good, sturdy pair of leather shoes is a basic requirement in the business arena. Glance down at any executive gathering and you'll note various styles of well-crafted, highly functional coverings for the feet: Some reflect the current fashion of the day — others are of a classic design. What you should also note, and research from The Protocol School of Washington® confirms, is that shoes are an important component of professional presence, silently broadcasting a great deal about their owner. So it is with manners.

Wise words from the eighteenth-century English statesman, Lord Chesterfield (Philip Dormer Stanhope), remind us that

> *Manners must adorn knowledge, and smooth its way through the world. Like a great rough diamond, it may do very well in a closet by way of curiosity, and also for its intrinsic value; but it will never be worn, nor shine, if it is not polished.*

Every diamond in the rough and every pair of shoes that carry us to a professional interview will surely benefit from the high gleam of polish! So it is with individuals. Extend your manners by writing personal notes, repeating silently to yourself three or four times that name you've just heard in an introduction, standing for all introductions, silencing your telephone before you enter a seminar, and presenting your business card with the writing facing the recipient. Add polish to your professionalism. Great manners make for great business!

ABOUT CECILIA B. GRIMES

Cecilia Grimes author, speaker, trainer, coach is a certified etiquette and protocol consultant. She travels throughout North America, working with individuals who want to present themselves with authority and confidence, and who wish to add more polish to their professionalism. Her clients include executives from Fortune 500 companies, athletes and coaching staffs, and professionals in the fields of engineering, law, banking and finance, academia, hospitality, and technology.

Cecelia is a native North Carolinian with an undergraduate degree from Wake Forest University and a masters from Duke University. She received her etiquette credentials at the prestigious Protocol School of Washington®.

Contact Information:
Cecilia B. Grimes
Etiquette Matters
513 W. Glendale Street
Siler City, NC 27344

Phone: (919) 742-3616
Fax: (919) 742-3616
E-mail: EtiquetteMatters@mindspring.com
Web: EtiquetteMatters.com

TOGETHER EVERYONE ACHIEVES MORE!

by Jerry and William Fritz

My oldest son, Will, is a member of the swimming, tennis and cross country teams at our local high school. His cross-country coach, Doug Debroux, uses the T E A M acronym, as in this chapter's title, as a way to motivate a select group of individual athletes. I took the opportunity to interview Coach Debroux regarding his philosophy/approach as well as question my son about his experiences and reflections on being a team member. Will's comments and insights can be found throughout this chapter and are designated by

(WF). I selected this example as a foundation for this commentary because it is one of the finest examples of team (business or athletic) discipline and motivation that I have ever come across. It is also a wonderful model for what needs to happen in businesses today. Here's just a brief example — as each member of this team crosses the finish line, he catches a second wind and heads back to the "funnel" (final 100 yards to the finish line) to help Coach cheer on his teammates.

After all have been duly congratulated and pats on the back have subsided, the discussion focuses on how the team placed in respect to their own PR (personal record — measurement of how well they achieved their goals for the meet). Throughout this text I will bold what I consider to be **Important Learnings** we should all pick up from the real-world example just offered. These are action items we all need to consider and they will be indicated as **IL**. Here is the first IL — **The visual/verbal support the team leader and other team members**

provide is one of the critical motivators that can focus a person or group on goal achievement.

The purpose of this chapter is not to cover all the variables that can impact a team's success but rather to use an everyday, real-life example, the Oregon High School cross country team and their coach, to highlight some of the most important aspects that drive a team/team leader to ultimate success. I am compelled at this juncture to sincerely thank Coach Debroux and my son for their time and wonderful insights. "Thank you both!"

What is a team?

Here is the definition developed by Jon Katzenbach and Douglas Smith that is frequently used by today's business world: "A team is a small number of people with complementary skills who are committed to a *common purpose*, set of *performance goals* and approach for which *they hold themselves mutually accountable.*"[1]

Back to the cross-country team as it relates to this definition. Let's address those four elements and offer examples of each. *Complementary skills* are developed by an ongoing program focused on the variables that need to be addressed for success, including each team member's personal development. (WF) There are many variables that impact the way you perform. One is hydration management. All through practices, Coach is always telling you to drink water. He knows that drinking lots of water is essential for the human body and muscles to work at an optimal level. You are also told not to drink pop, because the carbonation makes it harder to be active and does not provide what your body needs. *IL — Team leaders use their experience and expertise to guide the team members so they are adequately prepared for the tasks to come and show them the potential pitfalls that could lie ahead.* (WF) We also have progressive running training. We work on running longer and longer distances at practices, and then run them faster and faster. This type of training builds your muscles to be more powerful and also provides personal motivation, driving you to new limits you didn't think were possible. At the same time you also work on sprints after a long run to get in shape for surges during a race, and for the all- out sprint at the end. *IL — Training needs to come in spurts and each session should be progressive and built onto the previous. What is taught should directly relate to a specific activity or responsibility that the individual is being held accountable for.*

One of the observations I have made over these past ten years as a trainer, educator/observer and consultant — world-class organizations believe their employees are never trained but that they are always in training. And that, they say, is why they are leaders in their respective industries. All athletic teams obviously understand this avenue for success. Does your business practice this philosophy?

As you develop teams within your own organization, have you identified all the variables that will impact the individual and team success? Is there a plan to develop and grow the personal skills and attributes that focus on the overall team's ability to achieve success?

The second component of our working definition is often stated as the #1 reason why a team fails. There must be a clear and established goal for the team to aim for. Establishing a *common purpose* includes:

- Clarity of expected results
- Measurable, attainable and specific goals
- Team focus on continuous improvement
- Effective and consistent communication
- Establishing a trusting environment
- A cohesiveness among team members
- Belief that success can be achieved
- Knowing the "rules of the game"
- Competency in team leadership

(WF) Being part of a team is very different from being on your own. As a member of the Oregon Cross Country team, I know what it is like to be a part of a team. Even though running is a fairly individual sport, our coach looks at it as being all about the team. We sometimes have early morning practices before school. After these practices, there normally is some sort of team breakfast planned. This is so we have the energy to perform for the rest of that day in our schoolwork, but it also gives us time to form bonds of friendship with each other. We have spaghetti dinners the night before every meet. This gives us the nutrients we need to run better during the race, and is again a time for us to develop bonds. We also use this time to talk with each other about our personal goals and team goals for the upcoming meet. *IL — Though our work may be individually evaluated, it is the focus on overall team/department goals that leads to success. And it helps if we get to know our fellow team members in a social as well as business setting.*

(WF) We work as a team during everything we do. Even during the actual race we work in little teams of two or more runners. This has two effects: 1) we push each other to go faster and stronger than we normally would, and 2) a strong level of motivation is created, causing all of us to ultimately do much better than if we were running alone. *IL — The synergy of working side-by-side with someone you believe in and who believes in you is absolutely overpowering.*

The third quarter of our team definition is often left out or is minimally addressed. My observations suggest that we often tell people what to do, but we normally do not explain and show them just how well they must do their part.

A *set of performance goals* becomes the singular target on which everyone is focused.

These goals can include:

- The specific results the team is being asked to attain
- What skills you must practice
- How well you must practice the necessary skills
- Your specific contribution to the whole effort and how that contribution will be measured
- Expectations set forth by the team leader
- Expectations set forth by the team
- Your personal desires for continuous improvement

(WF) One thing we never say, though, is that we beat someone else on our team. That is one of the things Coach teaches you right from the start. You cannot beat someone who is on your team. This outlook helps keep everything positive. The reason you can't beat someone on your own team is that you function almost as a single entity. Saying that you beat someone on your own team is like saying you beat yourself. If we started competing against each other, that would stop the groups of team members from working together. More people would run alone and wouldn't do as well as if they were working with the group. Instead of talking about how we got a one-two finish (when two members of the same team finish first and second), we would be worrying about who got first. It would break up the oneness that makes our team so strong. So we cannot beat each other; we only happen to finish before them. *IL — In the absence of internal competition, everyone's actions are more supportive, team goals have a higher priority than individual goals, relationships grow stronger and mutual trust is evident.*

(WF) At the beginning of a season, Coach has us write down our goals for our first meet and for the season. Quite often, by the end of the season each of us has surpassed our goals by a lot. We wind up doing better than we thought we ever could because no one wants to fall behind the other. You support each other. In doing so, you go faster. Plus, if you are running with someone who has a higher goal than you, you tend to meet their goal with them, since you stick together. When you meet a goal midseason, you could decide to stay at that level, but the other members of the team won't let you stop at being less than you can be. They push you all the time and help you become better. They push you just by getting better themselves. You feel like if they are getting better, you should work to get better, too. You often end up with a new goal almost every meet as you improve. You feel a need to push yourself harder, to find your limit and then surpass it. And the entire team is there to help you, just as you are there to help all of them. It is like a form of peer pressure, but is completely positive. *IL — a) It is impossible to hit a target you cannot see, b) business goals are much too complex today to hit them all by yourself, and c) reasonable goals, though they may be quite a stretch, can and will be achieved if everyone helps each other.*

In *Psychology Today* a couple of years back there was an article describing how people learn. The final conclusion was that the majority of the population uses their five senses to draw information into the synapses of their brain. The breakdown is as follows:

1.5%	sense of smell
3%	sense of touch
1.5%	sense of taste
11%	sense of hearing
83%	sense of vision

Remember earlier when I said, "You cannot hit a target you cannot see?" Well, there you have it! *IL — For team success, it is very important that all goals and objectives are posted anywhere necessary to impact the #1 sense in how learning takes place.*

(WF) Our team has expectations of all of the members. These expectations are clear to everyone on the team because we get a sheet at the beginning of the season describing them and because Coach role models them (in both his athletic coaching and teaching). Throughout the year you see them on info sheets and on the marker board listing what we need for our next meet. They are constantly enforced and reinforced by each of the team members, not necessarily always from Coach. Some of these expectations include:

- we are expected to put our all into every race and practice
- we are expected to do what is right for ourselves to keep ourselves healthy
- attendance at practices or meets is not optional
- always ask the absolute best of your team members and yourself
- teach whatever you know to whoever can benefit
- look upon every experience as an opportunity to learn
- congratulate every other team member after every meet

- keep in mind what it took to get to where you are
- treat everyone the same with high respect and support

IL — Team expectations need to be clear and accepted by all. Some of the other competencies for business teams are:

> *All members:* developing others, customer service orientation, interpersonal understanding, oral communication, organizational awareness, organizational commitment, teamwork and cooperation, achievement orientation, initiative, analytical thinking, continuous improvement

> *Members only:* influence, adaptability, personal growth, self-control

> *Leaders only:* directing others, empowerment, team leadership, self-confidence, planning and organizing, conceptual thinking

The final component of Katzenback and Smith's definition is that team members *must hold themselves mutually accountable.* (WF) Another good thing about being part of the cross-country team is that you know you can always turn to the other members for help with almost anything. This continuous internal support allows you to feel comfortable with everyone. One of the big pluses about cross-country is that you always come out feeling good. If the team wins, you PR, or even if someone else PR's, you gain confidence. This is because if the team wins, that means that you helped them get to the victory, which makes you more confident. And if someone else PR's, even if you don't, you feel more confident because a member of your team is getting better. This then makes the team better, and in turn, you also become better. You obviously gain confidence in yourself when you PR, but you also gain confidence in the team because while you personally are getting stronger, you are helping to make the team stronger at the same time. This type of linkage between us creates an internal bond that cannot be broken, win or lose. *IL — You may have already seen the following. Whether you have or haven't, I firmly believe it can offer some tremendous insights on how to make teams more successful. Please read —*

Lessons from the Geese

Fact 1: As each bird flaps its wings it creates an uplift for the bird following. By flying in a "V" formation, the whole flock gains 71 percent greater range than if the bird flew alone.

LESSON: People who share a common direction and sense of community can get where they are going quicker and easier because they are traveling on the thrust of one another.

Fact 2: Whenever a goose falls out of formation, it suddenly feels a drag and resistance of trying to fly alone. It quickly moves back into formation to take advantage of the lifting power of the bird immediately in front.

LESSON: If we have as much sense as a goose, we will stay in formation with those who are headed where we want to go, and we will be willing to accept their help as well as give ours to others.

Fact 3: When the lead goose gets tired, it rotates back into formation, and another goose flies at the point position.

LESSON: It pays to take turns doing the hard tasks and sharing leadership. With people, as with geese, we are interdependent on each other's skills and capabilities.

Fact 4: The geese in formation honk from behind to encourage those up front to keep up their speed.

LESSON: We need to make sure that our honking from behind is encouraging.

Fact 5: When a goose gets sick or wounded or is shot down, two geese drop out of formation and follow it down to help and protect it. They stay with it until it is able to fly again or dies. They then launch out on their own with another formation or catch up with their flock.

LESSON: If we have as much sense as geese, we too will stand by each other in difficult times as well as when we are strong.

"Lessons from Geese" was transcribed from a speech given by Angeles Arrien at the 1991 Organizational Development Network and was based on the work of naturalist Milton Olson.

My consulting experiences have clearly validated that *Fact 4* above has a tremendous impact on personal and team success. (WF) It is a great feeling to have the entire team that is not running during your race, or who has already finished, cheering for you as you come to the finish. As you come in, other team members give you water, a wet towel to put on your head, and help support you both mentally (congratulations, etc.) and physically (help hold you up). And as soon as you get your feet back under you, you do the same for those who are still finishing.

Coach Debroux senses that this is one of the primary reasons for his team's success. "The encouragement the kids give each other weighs much more heavily than anything I say or do." Imagine the impact of everyone cheering each other. This kind of congratulation action is simply an affirmation that who people are and what they do matters and that they are making a valuable contribution toward achieving the shared *mission* — right work done the right way.[2]

"Catch people doing something right."[3] I have never forgotten this simple but most profound statement. It really does work, you know. *IL — The #1 motivator of employees across all industries is APPRECIATION FOR A JOB WELL DONE. When is the last time you made a positive comment to an individual about his performance? When did you last give someone a hand-written personal note congratulating them on their outstanding effort?*

Pride and Recognition

(WF) Another thing we get from cross-country is a sense of pride in our team and ourselves. When we get all of our people finishing the race, even when members of other teams are passing out, it makes the whole team feel proud. And you develop a major sense of pride in yourself for helping the team and for finishing yourself. There are times during the race that you feel like you just can't go on, but the thought of letting the team and yourself down by not finishing causes you to push on. During a couple of races during my 1999 season I had some knee problems in the middle of the race. At first I didn't think I would be able to finish, but the thought of letting the team down made me get up and get more determined. I finished every race I ran in the season and felt great for making what I know was a valuable contribution. *IL — Each employee must realize that the work they do is important and without each person's valuable contribution, neither the team nor the organization has any hope of achieving success.*

I have observed many different forms of recognition throughout my years of business analysis, and I must highly recommend Bob Nelson's *1001 Ways To Reward Employees* as one of the finest collections of real-world motivation examples ever assembled. You will find many unusual and common sense ways to get your team members pumped up and ideas on how to build an environment in which everyone will be dedicated to giving 110% consistently. Some of the other ideas I have seen successfully used include:

1. "Bragboards" where all the team accomplishments are posted for the rest of the organization to see

2. Reserved parking spaces for team member or team of the month

3. A catered meal with the team as guests of honor

4. A public thank you to the team during an organizational-wide meeting

5. Personal "thank you" letters to each member of the team, with a copy to the personnel file

6. Establish a club in your organization and induct teams who save the company significant amounts of money

7. Invite teams who make significant strides to present their success at a management team meeting

8. Host a field day for the team

9. Gift certificates for each member of the team to take his or her spouse out to a nice meal at a local restaurant

10. Spotlight in the organization's internal newsletter or communications piece highlighting the team's accomplishments

11. A day in which the sponsor agrees to be the team's "gopher" by running errands or helping the team members out with annoying details of their daily jobs

12. Plaques or certificates presented to the team by the sponsor and/or the sponsor's boss

13. "Caught Posters" identifying team member(s) who performed admirably as observed by their supervisor

(WF) At the end of the season we have a banquet for the entire team and their families. At this banquet we enjoy a pot-luck meal and engage in positive discussion about the season just finished. And then the evening concludes with our awards ceremony. Coach calls up each of the team members and describes, sometimes humorously, how they did through the season and about their accomplishments. This makes everyone proud, and when everybody cheers for you when he finishes talking, you realize just how appreciated you really were. We also show appreciation for the seniors because they have been the nucleus of the team, as well as our leaders. The final part of the night is a slide show, and this is the best of all. Set to our kind of music, there are pictures of our families and different shots taken throughout the season of the members. It is a great season ender, and it provides lots of motivation, making you want to have next season begin immediately. *IL — Celebration of individual and team successes is a major contributing factor to the perpetuation of forward focus and future success. One of the commonalities of world-class companies is that they celebrate their successes often.*

Some Closing Thoughts and Summary

(WF) We also have something called the warm down. This is the jog we take after a race to loosen our muscles and burn the lactic acid out of our muscles. During the warm down, we talk about how we did, and, if someone is feeling bad about how they did, we try to help them out. We point out the things they were doing right, and then what they did that can be improved upon. It isn't approached as their having done something wrong; it's that they could do better. It is also a time when most of the congratulations go around for the winners and those who got their PR that race. As a result it's not just a time to relax our muscles, but also to relax our minds from the extreme focus of the race to a broader view of how we all did. *IL — Continuous opportunities to debrief, offer congratulations and renew the spirit for future challenges create the synergy and motivation to continue on even when times are tough.*

(WF) Coach treats all of the runners on the team the same. No matter how good or bad, fast or slow you are, as long as you are trying, you are treated the same. This is great because it eliminates any bad feelings toward someone who got "special treatment" or something similar. This makes it a lot easier to get along with everyone on the team. Plus, almost everyone on the team goes on this same theory, so the seniors do not shun you because you are a freshman. *IL — Showing favoritism will create an incurable cancer within the team and will de-motivate even those not directly affected.*

What a pleasant surprise it has been as a parent observing a true team in action. Hearing Will talk about it around our dinner table and then seeing Coach's philosophy in action has been an eye-opening opportunity. Everything you have read in this chapter is completely usable in the business world. I am confident your team will improve dramatically if you take to heart the approach that Coach Debroux practices and begin utilizing the Important Learnings summarizing each major point.

It is a certainty in our highly competitive business world that utilizing the team approach is one of the surest ways to create a competitive advantage. Use the concepts you have read in this book so your organization can begin the journey of becoming a world-class organization. And, please remember, if you work the process as described in this chapter, **T**ogether **E**veryone (in your organization) will **A**chieve **M**ore!

Footnotes

1. Jon Katzenback and Douglas K. Smith, "The Discipline of Teams," *Harvard Business Review,* March-April 1993, p. 111.

2. Kenneth Blanchard and Sheldon Bowles, *Gung Ho!,* 1999.

3. Kenneth Blanchard and Spencer Johnson, *The One Minute Manager*, 1982.

ABOUT JERRY L. FRITZ

*J*erry Fritz has dedicated a lifetime to leading edge training in customer service and sales. With his trademark 120% energy and enthusiasm, he rose quickly from account representative to national accounts manager to manager of training and new business development to national sales manager to general manager with M.S. Carriers, Roto-Rooter Services Company, Catenation and North American Van Lines, Inc.*

For the past decade Jerry has been the Director of Sales and Customer Service Management program at the Management Institute, University of Wisconsin (Madison) School of Business. He is a featured speaker at conferences sponsored by Inc. magazine and those sponsored by The Customer Service Management Journal in both the U.S. and England. Jerry is a recent recipient of the Marketing Educator of the Year award by Sales and Marketing Executives International. He is the author or co-author of several books, including 19 Skills to WOW Your Customers.

Contact Information:
Jerry Fritz
800 Miller Drive
Oregon, WI 53575

Phone: (608) 835-9125
Fax: (608) 262-4617
E-mail: JLF@mi.bus.wisc.edu
Web: www.Wisc.edu/mi

TEAMWORK ACHIEVES CHECKERED FLAG RESULTS: LESSONS LEARNED ON THE HIGH-SPEED OVAL

by Renée Merchant

"I can't think of anything major that anyone has accomplished by themselves."

—Ned Jarrett, Winston Cup Champion,
Broadcaster and Business Owner

We live within four miles of the start/finish line of Michigan Speedway in the beautiful Irish Hills of southeastern Michigan. One of my favorite things to do is drive a competition stock car on the high-banked oval speedway, just for fun. This experience, getting into a stock car with only one seat and driving as fast as possible, seems solitary. But it takes a team of people to help me have an exciting experience. The Track Time instructors and auto mechanics, speedway support people, fire and ambulance crews all work together to make sure the driving participants have a safe, stimulating experience.

As a professional speaker/trainer/consultant and business owner, I cannot help but notice the similarities between competition auto racing and teamwork in the workplace. They both require a shared vision, short-term and long-term goals with people working at their fullest potential, overcoming barriers and seeking continuous improvement *together*. This takes teamwork, and this is what I have learned while driving a stock car.

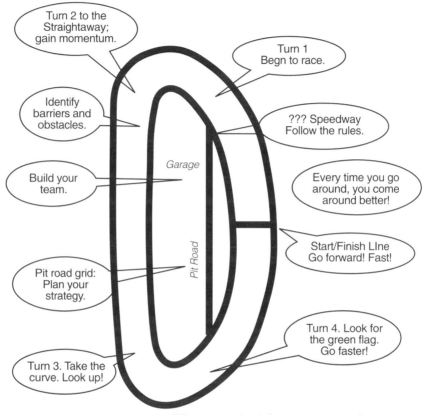

Where you look is where you will go!
Lessons Learned on the High Speed Oval

Prepare for TeamWork; It Starts in the Garage

Teamwork begins the moment you create your personal or professional vision for success. The vision is a statement that is specific, measurable, time-framed and exciting enough to inspire you to take action. The overall vision consists of manageable chunks of short-term and long-term goals. When all of these goals are reached, the vision is achieved. The race-car driver has the vision of winning the championship this year by finishing in at least the top five every time he or she races. In auto racing, the team goal is always "to be the first to take the checkered flag," that is, to win; but often just finishing well does much the same thing. Therefore, the short-term goal is finishing well in the next race; the long-term goal is winning the championship at season's end.

For business owners and managers, the vision might be to improve company sales 20 percent in the next six months by improving on-time delivery while maintaining quality. For community leaders, the vision might be to build an endowment fund of one million dollars within the next year to ensure the preservation of a local park for public use.

Although race drivers are out there on the track alone, he or she needs a team in the garage to put him there and a pit crew to keep him ahead of the competition. His team includes the auto mechanics, pit crew, sponsor advertisers, manufacturers, track and sanctioning body officials, and spectators. These entities support the drivers by providing skill, research, money, latest technology, physical strength, and applause to cheer them to victory.

Build Your Team

What resources, skills and knowledge do you require to be successful in achieving your vision? Do you need a specialized degree, new knowledge, or technical skills? Do you need a financial planner, a great salesman, or a well-organized staff person? Based on this analysis, start to build your team. Find people around you with these necessary skills and strengths, and ask them to join your team. Already, there are many people who want you to be successful. Your suppliers want you to buy more of their products/services, your customers want you to continue to provide excellent goods/services, and even your competitors see your success as a challenge to them to be better! Are any of these people willing to help you?

Where do you find team members? You network with other successful people in business. There are three major categories: vocational, professional and personal. You join a relevant professional association, a local business organization, or a service club. To gain specific skill or knowledge, take a class at community college or extension service of a major university. To practice your new skill, provide leadership to a professional association or community-oriented committee. To achieve a personal goal, join a health club or take a continuing education class. Tell people about your vision and let them hear your enthusiasm. Ask them to join your team by becoming your mentor or advisor. Form an informal advisory board to help you identify barriers, solve problems and develop opportunities for improvement.

On race teams, all participants share the overall team goal of "taking the checkered flag," but each achieves an individual vision by teaming with the driver. For example, the sponsor wants his advertising logo and colors to be seen by as many people for as long a time as possible. If the driver records a DNF (did not finish), then the sponsor loses valuable market visibility time on the track. The automobile manufacturer wants his automobile to be viewed as reliable, safe, and fast, because ultimately customers (purchasers of the vehicle) will see the street version as having the same characteristics. Success builds brand loyalty. The pit crew shares in the driver's success by celebrating in the winner's circle and receiving a monetary bonus.

For your team members, find out what their individual visions are. How do they measure success? Is it name recognition, power to influence and inspire others, or monetary rewards? Ask them how they view their success and determine how all of you can benefit by working together.

What will be the role of these new members of your team? What will be their responsibilities? The role of crew chief is to interface between the pit crew and the driver. The crew chief is responsible for providing accurate data to help the rest of the team make critical decisions. Identify your needs and help your team understand your expectations for working together. Do you expect your team members to serve as only a "sounding board" to your great ideas? Or, do you want your team to provide advice, options and suggestions? Or, do you want to delegate authority to them to make decisions for specific situations? You will need to be specific. In any case, you need to communicate how important their contribution is to your success.

Pit Road Grid: Plan Your Strategy

Together you plan the strategy. How will you communicate: what, when and how often? Race teams use radios in the car to communicate with the pit crew, owner and team member spotters (lookouts in the stands). While racing, they will discuss the strategy for the next planned pit stop, such as replacing only two tires instead of all four. The driver will describe how the car is handling so the pit crew can make any necessary chassis adjustments at that time. The spotter will warn the driver of an accident up ahead so he can take evasive action.

In addition, the track officials use a system of colored flags and lights to communicate track conditions. For example, in the case of an accident, they show the yellow flag, which communicates "caution, slow down." At the same moment, the pit crew prepares for a caution flag pit stop and is ready when the driver brings the car into the pits. The flags also communicate distance remaining in the race. For example, crossed flags signal "the race is half over" and a white flag communicates "one lap remaining."

How will you communicate with your team: face-to-face, e-mail, or telephone? How often will you speak together? You may set up a regularly scheduled meeting with your mentor at a mutually convenient time and place. For your informal advisory board, schedule a half-day meeting quarterly at a meeting room in a local restaurant and buy their lunch. Write "family time" into your schedule to be sure this part of your team is not neglected. Plan when you will take time out and return to the pits for rest and rejuvenation, a drink of water and four new tires.

The race team has an electronic database of experiences from previous races run in different weather conditions using various mechanical set-ups. What is your strategy for environmental scanning to spot potential pitfalls and identify new market opportunities? You may want to subscribe to an Internet service that searches and sorts topics and articles of importance to your business. Listen to people in your network who are willing to share their past experiences, successful and not so successful. Find out what they learned about these situations.

Look at every event as an opportunity to capture ideas and make them your own. For example, a lunchtime speaker at your service club may tell about her trip to a distant city. She mentions there are "no quick-oil-change garages like we have here." You see this as an opportunity to expand your franchise business. Great ideas are everywhere; we need only to keep our eyes open!

Ready to Race

You are ready to "go racing." You are dressed in a heavy, fire-resistant suit, gloves and a cumbersome helmet that restricts peripheral vision but will keep you safe. Your spotter will keep you informed of changing track conditions. There are the cars — lined up silently on the asphalt grid, shining brightly in the sun. The cars are painted blue, red, black, orange, and green: completely covered with advertising logos for tires, motor oil, ".coms" and aspirin. The mechanics have prepared a safe, fast car for you to drive. You climb into the seat and buckle the 5-point safety belt. You try to adjust the mirrors, but they are bolted in place. You try the gearshift, left foot on the clutch, right hand on gearshift, 1st, 2nd, 3rd, 4th gear. You have your vision in place for success in business and personal life. You are poised and focused. Your team is prepared to support you in the pits and celebrate with you in the winner's circle. Launch your vision by implementing the plan for your first goal.

Begin to Race: The Start/Finish Line

Flip the switch to start the engine. VROOOOM! You are surprised by the loud noise and anticipation of the moment. You know what to do — step on the accelerator, ease up on the clutch, shift! The driving instructors have prepared you well. You shift into gear and your years of experience take over automatically. You remember the rules of the road. Look for oncoming cars and move up onto the backstretch. Travel around the track getting a feel for the car. Drive to the start/finish line, and you see the flagman wave the green flag. You know all is in place, you are ready to take the risk and you step on the accelerator. "Go, go, go!" You are living your vision.

Green Flag — Go!

Turn 1 — Resist the temptation to slow down. Momentarily, you hesitate, unsure about this new experience. Your instructor told you the 18° banking would help you maintain your speed and line. You built this team; now trust this team. Look down to the left for the large, orange cone between turns 1 and 2. This is a guidepost and a welcome sight. It is something familiar to point you to the next task. When you reach the cone, you remember the instructor's words, "Look *up* and to your right for the mark in turn 2. It's a difficult thing to do. But where you look is where you will go." You look up.

Turn 2 — You see the concrete wall. This huge barrier is just waiting for you to make a wrong move and slam into it at 140 mph. Your business shows early signs of success and you charge ahead, only to be confronted with something you did not foresee, a new competitor entering the marketplace. You radio your team for guidance. A new competitor will challenge you to go faster. The team gives you data and options. But your personal experience clicks in again, and you do not let this barrier deter you from your goal. You take a deep breath, face the wall and adjust your position to avoid it. You experience short-term success, and there ahead of you is the straightaway. Go faster!

Yellow Flag — Caution!

Something unexpected has happened on the track in front of you and the flagman shows the yellow flag. Ahead, another car is spinning in front of you, and, instinctively, you take evasive action. You slow down and go low on the track. In business, the cautionary event could be an equipment failure that results in poor quality or a slow-down in production. You risk giving poor service to your customer because you did not stick to the preventive maintenance plan. Or, it could be that your supplier had a "fire in the garage" that delays on-time delivery to you. Or, it could be great news — a big order from a new customer that will overwhelm your resources. The team helps you discover a solution to get you back on track. You slow down briefly to regroup and then push the accelerator again, bringing you back up to speed.

Where You Look is Where You Will Go!

Turn 3 — no hesitation this time. You trust the banking will help to maintain your speed and position, safely. The speedway developers built a safe environment for you to do business. The economy is stable and there are numerous opportunities to grow. You are in control and you make the decision to move forward. You see the next indicator: the orange cone guidepost between turns 3 and 4. You head for it confidently.

Turn 4 — look up for the marker. You remember the words of your instructor, "Where you look is where you will go!" You look to your goal, the start/finish line, and there it is straight ahead. The track official waves the green flag again. You see clear, open road as you cross the line. One lap is completed. This is a milestone for your business. You have experienced a successful launch. There are no obstacles and no barriers in sight. You go as fast as you can, faster than ever before.

Black Flag — Penalty

You are doing so well that you push the team and yourself too hard. A missed gear change or business mistake can result in your facing the penalty flag. The temptation here is to pull over and call it a day. It is easier to go back to the garage, pack up and go home. Remember that the only people who do not make mistakes are those people who are standing still. You are the driver, the team leader; it is up to you admit the mistake, learn from it, and move forward.

Crossed Flags:
Time for Reflection and Course Correction

The flagman shows you crossed flags — a signal you are halfway to goal completion. This is a good time to reflect on your progress to this point. What have you learned to help you be better next time? Document your learning so you will build an archive of business conditions and your actions. What potential problems has your environmental scanning identified? Do you need new team members with different expertise? Are there new resources, skills and knowledge you need to continue your success? Does your team have all it needs from you to be success-ful? What can you do in your business and personal life to improve your position?

Every time you go around, you come around better!

As in business, some tasks we repeat over and over, almost by rote. Some people think auto racing is a waste of time because you go around in a circle and never go anywhere. But they miss the point. On the speedway, as you go around again and again, with every lap you try to improve your line and your speed. This is exactly what you do in business when you strive to improve quality, productivity, and customer service. Every time you go around, you come around a little better. This is the Cycle of Continuous Improvement. What opportunities await you at the next turn? How can you capitalize on these and make success happen for you? Take the time to review your measures of success and your track record. Identify the fluctuations and variances. Determine the cause for these and plan actions to make improvements.

You take the white flag — one lap to finish, and this is your last chance to push yourself to the limit. You push the accelerator to the floor. No easing up this time. The flagman shows the checkered flag and your run is complete. You have achieved one goal on your road to success. You slow down to move onto the apron to enter the pit road, just as race car drivers do. You are thrilled with the feeling of achieving a once-in-a-lifetime goal, and you did it all by yourself! But there, waiting for you is your team; the people who helped you have a successful run. No stock car driver or business leader could achieve anything without a team ready to help in the pits or give support back in the office.

Celebrate!

Standing in the winner's circle, you remember to thank your team-mates who helped you achieve your success. You want them to go around with you again next time. While this was only a short-term goal (a checkered flag finish), many of these add up to be the long-term goal—the championship and your vision! How will you celebrate this great feeling of success? That feeling happens only when there is teamwork and you have achieved synergy. It is true. The whole is greater than the sum of its parts. No one succeeds alone; we need the team working together.

"You can have the fastest engine, most aggressive driver, and best skilled pit crew, but if they ain't working together as a team, you've got nothing."

— Richard Petty,
NASCAR Winston Cup Champion and Car Owner

ABOUT RENÉE MERCHANT

Renée Merchant works with leaders and teams who want a faster way to build high-performance teams and with team leaders who want to reenergize existing teams. She founded DELTA SYSTEMS in 1982 and is a professional speaker, trainer and organization development consultant. Renée is highly regarded in business and industry for her dynamic, interactive programs that achieve results. Her clients include Ford Motor Company, Visteon, Tenneco Automotive, Detroit Edison and Fermi 2 Nuclear Power Plant. Renée is the creator of CARStyles™ Communication Style Model and the co-author of Checkered Flag Teams: The Fastest Way to Build Teams.

Renée and her husband, Dick, are active volunteers in their community to raise money for scouting, handicapped children's programs and a local hospital. And they are both avid auto-racing fans.

Contact Information:
Renée Merchant
DELTA SYSTEMS
5621 Somerset Drive
Brooklyn, MI 49230

Phone: (517) 592-5463
Fax: (517) 592-5463
E-mail: Renee@4DeltaSystems.com
Web: www.4DeltaSystems.com

YOUR TEAM CAN BE
YOUR LIFESAVER

by Mary Bryant

"If you want something done right, you've got to do it yourself!"

Growing up in a large family, I realized early that everyone always seemed busy with a personal agenda. At a young age, I decided that since no one else had *my* vision, I was the only person possible to accomplish things in a way I felt was successful. I knew how things should be — and no one else could match my efforts. I was very stubborn and self-sufficient.

As I grew older and became involved in organizations, I remember being told to delegate. But when I did, I felt assignments weren't done right, if they were done at all. I continued to take the lead, do things my way, and just let everyone else follow.

I went through life, attacking project after project, on committees, in the office, even at home, overwhelming myself with tasks and monumental lists of "to do's"— until one day, when God decided it was time for me to stop.

Breathe.

It was time to recognize that I am not the only one with potential in my selfish world. There are other people who could be valuable assets to myself and others, if only they had the opportunity.

My first eye-opening lesson came from my oldest brother, Don.

Part of this chapter is excerpted from *Underneath My Clothes* by Mary Bryant, a revealing look at the internal and external struggles in life.

Who is Don?

It was a cold evening in early January 1971. Dad was downstairs at his cluttered work table, sorting through the endless piles of bills. Mom was working late at the hospital. My younger sister and I were taking down the Christmas tree, and my three older brothers were doing the dishes. At least that's what they were *supposed* to be doing.

The boys were running circles through the house; chasing after each other while flipping towels. All of a sudden, there was a loud crash! My oldest brother Don tripped on the plastic runner which led to the sliding glass doors of the back patio. He grabbed onto a dining chair, cut his lip on the china cupboard and fell to the ground.

Don was instantly paralyzed from the neck down. He was only sixteen years old.

Don spent a *lot* of time in hospitals. When he was home, Mom had us take turns helping out. Occasionally, we'd get some professional help with home aids, physical therapists, and tutors. My parents were told he would never walk again.

With so many complications and emergency trips to the hospital, he never did finish high school, drive a car, or have a job or a date.

Don never complained, but he required a lot of time and attention. As a family, we had to work as a team to tend to his every need. He needed to be fed. He needed medication. He needed someone to help him blow his nose!

I was just a young girl. I wanted someone to pay attention to me. I incessantly tried to escape this situation. I wanted to play. I wanted to go swimming at the high school, where the boys were. I wanted to be in the Girl Scouts, so I could feel normal — like "one of the girls."

Several years later, when I turned fourteen years old, I became involved in modeling. It wasn't long before I got caught up in the dangerous, self-centered bubble world of *me, me . . . me!*

As I progressed in my career, so did the pressure. My eventual move to New York City brought on even stricter requirements. The modeling industry creates a ridiculous demand to be extremely thin. I remember constantly struggling with my figure — to look even *better*. I strived to be the best I could be. I decided running might give me that popular lean, trim body.

One morning, I put on my shoes and headed out the door. I got about two blocks! Huffing and puffing, feeling what most of us would describe as lung burn, I was convinced that *I couldn't run*. Then it hit me — like a big solid brick in the head.

I have a brother who couldn't walk out the door — who couldn't scratch his own nose. Yet Don smiled every day because he *could*.

I *could* run. I just didn't want to do the work!

Don became my inspiration. It was the beginning of a whole new world for me. There was life outside of my own selfish bubble. With time and training, I was able to feel stronger and run farther distances. In November of '94, I put Don's picture on two T-shirts. I sent one to him in Cleveland, Ohio, where he lives with our parents. I wore the other one and covered all five boroughs, 26.2 miles of the New York City Marathon!

It was never initially a goal to run a marathon; I just wanted to be able to eat, look good, and keep my job. I achieved *more* than I ever thought possible.

I continued to break open my self-sufficient bubble world.

Don became so special to me — I started to think about him, and his life. Twenty-five years after Don's fall in our Cleveland home, over seventy surgeries later, he continued to smile every day. Don became my model in life.

One night, in December of 1996, I lay awake in my bed, thinking about Don. I was moved by his physical battle that didn't mar his courageous spirit. Inside, I felt we were losing him. His fragile body had finally been through enough. I pulled together my resources and connections and began to shoot a documentary, capturing him and his spirit while I could.

As soon as the camera crew walked in the door a few days later, Don felt important. His health and strength perked up, like the birth of a new baby!

I began to dream of all the possibilities. Don uses a motorized wheelchair so that when he pushes his head into the headrest — the chair moves forward. Wouldn't it be cool — if he could join me on the racecourse! Don loved the idea.

There was incredible excitement and anticipation as we signed up for the local Cleveland Revco 10K that spring. It was only 6.2 miles, so I felt confident. We practiced a couple of times in the neighborhood.

I called my producer and director from Chicago — to tell them they *must* come back and cover this. They arrived the night before and became concerned when they looked at my brother.

Don sat in his chair, hunched over, glasses sliding down his nose. Not the picture of what would be considered an athlete.

"How many times has he gone six miles?" my producer Barbara asked.

I chuckled, and explained that he has only gone around the

driveway. It's a documentary — and Don *wanted* to try, so whether he goes five hundred feet or more — just shoot it.

That night — after witnessing the looks on their faces — I started to toss and turn. What was I doing? Is this dangerous? Could something happen to him while we were out in the crowd?

The next morning, Don was beaming with excitement, and his smile glared bigger than ever before. Our sister, Carolyn, artistically painted our names across matching royal blue sweatshirts. On the left knee of our sweatpants it read: "Run and roll with Revco, May 4, 1997." Dressed and fed, our family and crew loaded up and went downtown.

We decided it was safer to start in the back of the pack.

The gun went off, and we were on our way! Soon we realized that the very headrest that controlled the movement of the chair wasn't always helpful. With every bump and chuck hole in the road, Don's head would be thrown to the right or left — directing the chair right — and then left. Frequently, the bar against his cheek would get bumped, throwing the chair into reverse! Time after time we had to stop the chair, reset the gear, and start again. It was truly a test of patience.

Even the best thought-out plans will suffer setbacks and frustrations.

Three miles into the race, Don asked if we were almost done. My heart sank.

"Are you tired? Do you want to quit?" I asked him.

"No — let's just keep going" Don answered.

Soon, we rounded the last bend on the public square in downtown Cleveland. As we headed up Euclid Avenue, the crowds slowly began to cheer. Their intensity grew as we neared the finish line.

As I looked over at Don, I saw something more brilliant than I ever could have imagined. The smile of a man, my brother, who for the first time, in over twenty-five years, was doing something for himself. It was the most beautiful run of my entire life. I was filled with an emotion that I hope people everywhere would experience at least once in their lifetimes.

We crossed that finish line and the local news cameras rushed over. "What's next?" they grilled.

Don, exhausted from the one-hour and forty-five-minute trek, slowly announced, "The twenty-six miles of the NYC Marathon."

It seemed like I had created a monster. That night Don was featured on "Sports Sunday." I saw how giving one person an opportunity could make an incredible difference to so many.

The Jump Rope

My parents worried about Don. He constantly talked about going to New York City and attempting the Marathon. They felt it was impossible but didn't want to disappoint Don.

"Couldn't we just finish the documentary?" They kept asking me.

When I was a little girl — Don used to twirl the jump rope for me. We'd tie one end to the garage door handle, and he would twirl the other end, sometimes for hours at a time. I knew it was MY turn to twirl the jump rope for Don.

I fought legal, social, and medical battles. They did *not* want a power chair in the NYC Marathon. Don would lose home health care if he crossed state lines. No one was sure what his body could even handle. I wrote letters, made phone calls, had meetings with doctors, officials, the wheelchair corporation — and most importantly — I prayed. Mom and Dad were ready to kill me! I insisted I had put it in God's hands and then prayed some more.

On November 1, 1997, Don joined me at the start line of the NYC Marathon.

When I reminded him that we had gone only six miles before — and this was twenty-six miles — it would take all day — Don replied, "Well then, I'd better take my lunch box!"

Never did we focus on problems — only the possible solutions. We removed the lever which put the chair into reverse and had our friend Greg, an officer with the US Coast Guard, join us as part of the team. Any guy would love this kind of adventure. Maps, tools, walkie-talkies, and the camera crew in a jeep up ahead.

We ventured out across the Verrazzano Bridge and then into Brooklyn. My best friend Karla and her husband were assigned a difficult task: escort Mom and Dad to a point early in the course to cheer us on, then deliver them to the finish line. With them out of our way, we would be on our own. According to Don, the best part was going through red lights and not getting a ticket. What a day!

Everything was going smoothly; we were even ahead of schedule, until it began to rain — and thunderstorm. We were told the battery would work fine in wet weather, but I was concerned about Don. I added my rain poncho on his lap and asked him what he wanted to do.

"Let's just keep going," was his persevering reply.

So we did, for six hours and thirty-three minutes.

We did what *no one* thought was possible!

For over twenty-six miles, Don pushed his head into the headrest of his chair, and became the *first* man without use of his arms and legs to enter and complete the NYC Marathon.

It gave him such a boost that Don is still alive over two-and-a-half years later!

"Let's just keep going!" — Don became my hero.

What might happen if *you* gave someone a chance?

Is there someone in your life that *you* may have overlooked? Is there potential you may not have seen? Is there something *you* can do — or a team that can be developed to promote cooperation, rather than competition — to help someone shine?

My next lesson came from those who were inspired by my brother. It didn't take long, though, to realize that the value could be more tremendous to the leader than the team.

After my brother Don had opened the door for disabled athletes in powered chairs to participate in the NYC Marathon, I embraced the opportunity to coach the first wheelchair team, through the Achilles Track Club.

We headed out in Central Park on Tuesday evenings and created a convoy. What joy I had to see the faces of so many others, who never thought they would have the chance to do much of anything, let alone a marathon that fall. I relished my time with them — I felt I gave them life, the way I had done for my brother Don.

I remember one woman who dressed very simply. She had a blanket over her lap, covering her withering legs. Soon, she would come to practice, with a new added touch each week. She was so tickled that she had a Ford model as her coach. At first, I noticed the small beaded bag. That's when it hit me — this is really a special occasion for her! The following week, she started to wear eye shadow! Bright blue, painted all the way across her lids, from the tips of her lashes to her eyebrow. She had somewhere to go!

I couldn't help but wipe the tear in my eye before she could see me. I didn't want anyone to view me as emotional or "weak." I guess that's one of those "manly" traits that affect you when you're a leader. I'd just get them all fired up — "OK — let's go for an aerobic moment! — breathe in — breathe out!" Most of them had very limited use of their arms, so even warm-up stretches were a challenge. But we tried!

We'd check for speed, proper braking, wheel alignment, and battery life. I needed to be sure we were aware of every item that needed attention. I learned from Don: Think ahead. Create all possible solutions for all possible problems.

Then, something else took my attention.

On June 1, 1998, I was diagnosed with breast cancer. Young and healthy, a marathoner in my 30's, I was stunned. With a tumor that was almost 7 cm I had no choice but to have a mastectomy. My left breast, along with twenty-eight lymph nodes, was removed. It was traumatic on my body, not to mention my mind and spirit. My life was being taken away from me.

Even though my medical team technically saved my physical life, the greatest team was the one that saved my emotional and spiritual life, which I believe is at the core of all humanity.

Life went on —

Following surgery, I had a period of six weeks that I couldn't run. What an inconvenience to my schedule! I was a busy person with things to do, places to go, people to see. Most importantly, I had a marathon in four months, and a team to get to the start line.

My oncologist scheduled me for six months of chemotherapy; toxic chemicals to be put into my body. CMF (Cytoxin, Methotrexate, and 5FU) were administered every three weeks, directly into my veins. The toxins were cumulative. With each treatment, the side effects became worse.

I began to tell myself I was going for "spa" treatments. We were "cleansing" my body of that nasty cancer stuff. I needed to believe I could be filled with life as a result of these combined efforts.

I was nauseous, dizzy, sometimes confused in my thinking, and often fatigued. I kept going, but now I was struggling with two and three miles! It was a constant battle for strength. I received my treatments as scheduled, until ten days before the marathon. I went in to get some blood work and receive my chemotherapy. Dick Traum, president and founder of Achilles, and now my friend, even escorted me to make sure all was OK.

"Your white blood cell count is too low — we can't give you the chemo. You just aren't strong enough."

I couldn't believe what I heard. I felt pretty good — but the reports said differently. After a consultation with my oncologist, we decided to rest and take it easy for a few days and then we'd try one more time. Concerned with the side effects that are most prominent immediately following the treatments, I was hoping to have a longer recovery period before heading out on marathon day. But it just wouldn't be that way. So

I left the cancer treatment center depressed more than ever before, and went home to rest. I felt defeated.

The following week, just days before the marathon, I went back again to the cancer treatment center for my fifth round of chemotherapy. I had been praying, and so were family and friends. This time, the count was up enough to get my CMF. For the first time, I was actually excited to get chemo! I felt as though my body was getting stronger, healthier, and everything was going to be OK.

Then I heard something from my doctor that put me back on a downward spiral.

"If it's below 20° — or raining — you can't go."

"WHAT? — I CAN'T GO?" Oh NO! That's the last thing my survivor mentality wanted to hear! I HAD to be there. I felt as though I was striving, to give life to these people who were on our team. Seeing the joy and extended life it offered my brother, I wanted to see others experience this chance too. And the weather was something I could not control. I believed the team needed me, so again, I prayed.

Finally, the big day.

I woke up after a restless night, tossing and turning, remembering the months and months of planning and preparation. Don wasn't well enough to be there, but his spirit was. We were "Don's Team!" Extra batteries, customized warm yellow jackets, hats, and pennants had arrived. Every precaution was made to ensure the safety of everyone on the team. Each wheelchair athlete had been assigned at least one, if not two volunteers to personally ensure that needs were taken care of throughout the course. I even had a volunteer assigned to me! I promised the doctors and my mother that I would pull out if I had to, but I needed to be there to at least get them started.

It was a cold, dark, early November morning in 1998. I arrived at our meeting point. Almost everyone was already there. Each wheelchair member was carefully loaded up, and across the side of the bus a couple of volunteers had draped a "Don's Team!" banner.

I climbed aboard and in one glance I saw a sea of yellow jackets and smiling faces peeking out from underneath the uniform caps. Everyone glowed with anticipation of the day ahead. We were really doing this! I was so proud of them. I was so proud of my brother Don. I began to cry. I felt my strength being drained, and knew I had to toughen up. How far was I going to be able to take them? All I knew was that I felt God's presence with us. Even our bus driver was named Don!

Determined, we headed to the start line.

The gun went off — adrenaline carried all of us as we started over the first of five bridges. I couldn't help but think of Don, back home in Cleveland. Then it dawned on me; I had a cell phone! We all paused to call Don, so we could let him know — we were *all* there for him! Mom answered the phone. I asked her to put Don on the line. She obviously was caught up in her housework — "Oh Mary, I'm busy doing the dishes."

"Mom — I'm busy running a marathon with the wheelchair team. Can you just put Don on the line?"

Everyone was so patient — finally Don was on the phone, and after a count to three, we all shouted out in unison, "We love you Don!"

What a feeling that surged among us. There was a bond like no other. We took away the element of competition and brought in a spirit of cooperation. That's when I realized what had been lost in my life: Focus on the proper perspective.

You should have heard the members of the team, "How are you doing?" — "Are we going too fast for you, Mary?"

They cared about *me*! What a turnaround. The team didn't need me as much as I needed the team. Together, we continued along the course.

That day, just six days after my fifth round of chemotherapy, I joined "Don's team" in the NYC Marathon. When I couldn't run, I walked.

And I finished!

Success isn't always measured in a standard format. I believe that God gives each one of us a purpose and different strengths. When we accept each other and truly work as a harmonious team, those strengths flourish. Success is a team effort. No one succeeds alone.

When you're going through a tough time, do something for someone else. It's amazing the power it will give you!

ABOUT MARY BRYANT

*M**ary Bryant, a Ford model in New York City, is known as the "Model Who Can Speak." She is a board member of U.S. Wheelchair Sports Fund, received the Albert H. Gordon Award and was named Female Achilles Athlete of the Year. She travels across North America delivering a dynamic message about balanced success in your career, relationships, health and spirituality.*

Mary is the producer of Don's Story: The Smile of an Angel, *a documentary about the life and effect of her brother Don's spirit on others. Author of* Under My Clothes: Learning to be Comfortable with the Naked Truth, *Mary describes the laughter and tears of trying to keep a man, a job and her body. In her revealing memoirs, she shares lessons learned and her winning approach to success, happiness and life balance. Millions have gained hope and confidence through her keynotes, television appearances and print media. Mary has appeared on* CBS This Morning, EXTRA, Live with Regis & Kathie Lee, *and has been interviewed in* USA Today, New York Times, Crains' New York Business, SELF *and* Fitness.

Contact Information:
Mary Bryant
Bryant Enterprises
300 West 55th Street
New York, NY 10019
Phone: (212) 262-5004
Fax: (212) 262-5004
E-mail: BryantEnt@aol.com
Web: www.Mary-Bryant.com

Swords, Shields, Daggers and Handshakes: Having Power in Conflict

by Patti Wood, M.A., CSP

Your clients and customers are complaining, your e-mails are piled up like five o'clock traffic, and your to-do list is looking as ominous as the national debt. So what other great test of human strength and fortitude do you need to add to your day? How about those little tidbits of "helpful" criticism and negative comments from your teammates. Yes, those people hidden most of the day behind the cubical walls — the ones who are supposed to support you. Could this be their group motto — "one for all, all for one and pass the ammunition"? Sometimes it seems that your teammates are there to test you. Somehow they make your work day seem like a "Three Stooges" episode, and you're the one who keeps getting it in the eye.

What can you do? Is conflict with your teammates inevitable? I don't think so.

Granted, situations that can cause conflict are inevitable. But whether you turn that situation into a battle or an opportunity for growth is up to you. If you think conflicts are just part of the job and assume that a hostile attitude goes with the territory, you will face each day with two certainties: traffic and work-place conflict.

You may be thinking, "But you don't know my teammates, especially . . ."

You're right. I don't know them, but you do, and tomorrow when you go to work, they will still be there, waiting for you with a coffee cup and a sneer, ready to attack. What will you do?

If you are constantly dealing with criticism and negative

comments, you do have an option. You can follow these steps and turn the situation around:

Positive Steps To Power in Conflict

- Figure out how you typically respond
- Decide whether your current response is working
- Recognize that you have a choice of responses
- Uncover your style(s) Sword, Shield, Dagger, Handshake
- Understand the real source of the conflict
- Utilize the Handshake responses to deal with conflict

When you saw the words "Swords" and "Daggers" in the title of this chapter, you might have thought "All right! I'll learn how to get her good!" Sorry to disappoint you. You're not going to learn assault techniques. Put the tank in park and put away that M-16. Swords and Daggers are the old tools. Instead, you'll learn how to use "Handshakes" or non-defensive tools, so you can act rather than react. Instead of learning how to control others, you'll learn how to control yourself.

I'm not saying that you have to be 100 percent comfortable hearing negative information. This method isn't about being Pollyanna, smiling through the pain and thinking that everything is peachy keen. Nor is it about being a stooge waiting to get the pie in the face or a poke in the eye. You can learn to handle conflict constructively; you can learn to have personal power.

Step one: How do you typically respond?

The first step in having personal power in conflict is to figure out how you typically respond to criticism, negative messages and information in general that you don't want to hear. Realize that different situations and different people may evoke different responses. Let's explore the ways you protect yourself. What "Swords," "Shields" and "Daggers" do you use to keep from getting hurt when you feel under attack?

Think back to recent situations or even a situation from the past. How did you respond to verbal attacks, negative comments or criticism?

List as many reactions and responses as you can. (NOTE: Don't skip this step. It's important! Stop now and write. If you don't want to write here, get a separate piece of paper — but write.)

1. _____
2. _____
3. _____
4. _____
5. _____
6. _____
7. _____
8. _____

Okay, now look at your list. Do you leave the room, stuff down your feelings, raise your voice, give an excuse, counterattack, sabotage their next project, slam doors, go on the offensive with your own criticism, or ignore it and hope it will go away? Do you figure, "This guy doesn't know what he's talking about" or do you feel that you have to just grin and bear it? Do you go tell another teammate, tell your team leader, get busy or avoid seeing the negative teammate? Perhaps you postulate, "If this guy just did his job and didn't bother me I wouldn't have this problem." Do you take a break, get a headache, cuss up a storm, or lie awake at night and think about it? Do you get mad at yourself or go get a cup a coffee, thinking all the while, I'm right, you're wrong? Do you make plans with other teammates in the break room to get 'em at the next meeting, do you cry, eat something sweet or get quiet? Do you go home and complain to your spouse, or decide it's just not worth the time and aggravation? Do you make plans to mete out revenge sometime later? Do you sit at your desk or stand at your workstation thinking, "This always happens to me"?

If you said "Oh, yes!" to any of the above and they weren't on your list, or they made you think of new things, add them to your list now.

Surprise! All the things you just listed are defensive options. That makes perfect sense. You feel attacked, and you defend yourself. Negative information hurts. You have an image of yourself and you will go to great lengths to protect it. We all want to think "I am a good person" (however we define "good"), and when something happens to shake our core image of ourselves we get out the Swords, Shields and Daggers.

Remember, we called these forms of protection. And actually, you should feel good that you have developed these ways of coping in the world. You should be proud that you have survived. I'm not joking. You should feel good that you have devised skills to protect yourself.

Step two: Are your current response(s) working?

Now, ask yourself this question "Are these protections working well for me right now, everyday, in my interactions with my team-mates?" More importantly, what are the results of these interactions? Your protective behaviors might make you feel better temporarily, but are there ultimately costs to you? To the other person? To the team?

Do you feel that you've accomplished anything after a conflict? Perhaps your protective measures are not working as well as they used to, or maybe not with some people, or maybe they drain you of valuable energy that could be put to better use elsewhere.

Realistically, many of these responses may be appropriate in certain situations. For example, sometimes the best thing to do is to walk away from a conflict or just accept it even if it's not correct. But if you have a response you are using over and over again and it's not working, then it will be helpful to explore your patterns in order to discover some new options.

Step three: Recognize you have choices!

To begin to see that you have choices, go back to your list. Across from each item, write out its opposite. For example, if you wrote "Get mad," write across from it "Stay calm." If you wrote, "Leave the room," write across from it, "Stay and discuss the issue." (Stop and do that now.)

Not all the alternatives you write on the right side of the page are non-defensive and some of the responses on your original list may already be non-defensive. This exercise is to let you see what the alternatives are and help you realize you have a choice every time you are in a conflict. I'll say it again — you have a choice. The next time you are dealing with a conflict take a deep breath and ask yourself, "What's another way I could respond?"

As you look at the non-defensive opposites, you may say, "That would never work" or "I don't know how to make that work." Good news, you can learn how to use the non-defensive "Handshake" choices that will work and will leave you feeling positive instead of embattled. If you have some things on your list that you think are non-defensive, then you may already be using Handshakes. If you listed things on your left side list like "listening" and "asking questions," reward yourself immediately! Go out and buy yourself a really nice car, take a trip to Paris or just whisper quietly to yourself, "I knew I was smart."

Step four: Uncover your style(s).

There are four major styles of responding to conflict: Swords, Shields, Daggers and Handshakes. Below, I have defined each style and offered examples. As you read each one, ask yourself, "Do I do this? When and with whom?" Look at your original list carefully. You may see examples of a particular style or different styles. Sometimes, it's hard to recognize your real style because you have been using it for so long you think of it as your personality. Remember, as you go through the styles, be gentle with yourself. You are a good person, these styles have worked for you, and they may continue to be the best choice in some situations.

Swords

Swords use assertive and competing behavior. Their underlying belief is, "I'm more important than anybody else" and "My needs come first." This person may be seen by others as aggressive or even bullying. If you are a Sword wielder, you may see your behavior as a way to get things done and matters taken care of. In the extreme, Sword wielders attack the people who they feel wronged them or bystanders who get in the way. Countering criticism with criticism, yelling, getting angry, any phrase that starts with "Your mother . . ." is Sword behavior.

Sword wielders are out in the open, and they are direct. They don't hide their feelings. When someone uses a Sword, the body and voice communicate power.

Typically, a Sword wielder gets bigger; he takes up more space, perhaps standing with his legs farther apart. His heart is exposed, maybe even puffed up with the arms typically away from the heart. And the voice communicates power, perhaps with volume. The seemingly laid-back posture of a team member who leans back in her chair, arms above her head, fingers interlaced, elbows out, feet propped up on the desk, is indicative of a Sword wielder. This is called the "cape and crown posture." The "cape" is made by the arms above and the elbows out, making the head appear bigger. The crossed hands, with the fingers interlaced, is the symbolic crown. The feet up symbolically say, "I could step on you if I wanted to."

Shields

People who use Shields are unassertive. They can use either avoidance or accommodating responses. A Shield holder's underlying motivation is to get along and not get hurt. They can be passive in their responses, but may be viewed by you as "being nice" or "being a good team member." At their extreme, the Shield holder hides or cringes in response to negativity. "Woe is me . . . the poor victim," or "I'm a nice person, I never get mad."

Shield responses include avoiding the team member who is causing the problem, getting busy, laying the blame on someone or something else, giving a reason or an excuse, thinking that you somehow have to take it or put up with it, getting sick in response to conflict so the team members feel pity, complaining to your friends on the team about it but not the offending person, getting a headache or getting mad at yourself or saying "yes" to everything. Take note, saying "yes" or "you're right" when you are secretly thinking of how you're going to get them back later is a "Dagger" response. The nonverbal communication of a Shield holder shows a lack of power. Typically, the person takes up less space, the heart is protected, the hands may even cover the heart, the head might be lowered, direct eye contact is avoided, the voice may soften.

Daggers

People who use Daggers, or more specifically "Armor and dagger" behaviors, are a combination of unassertive and aggressive responses. An Armor and Dagger responder acts to protect himself or herself from harm and then strikes the offender later with a hidden Dagger.

Examples include saying "Yes" to a team member in a meeting and then not doing the task; responding to a negative comment with an ambiguous e-mail; smiling and letting your team leader think you're their friend but badmouthing them all the time to others on the team; or stuffing emotions but then showing displeasure subtly; or doing something a team member requested you not do and not telling them.

These behaviors are sometimes the most difficult to recognize in yourself. The secret is to look at your underlying motivations and emotions. The Armor maneuver is a way of saying "I'm not strong enough; I can't let my true emotions show." The hidden Dagger symbolically says, "I am angry or resentful, but you don't know. You'll get it eventually."

Daggers may rationalize that stuffing it until later is a good thing, but if they use it for ammunition later it is a defensive response. The Dagger user may think that going to tell other team members about an offender is a Shield response or even a positive response because he or she didn't let his anger show to the other person. But if the story is shared with the intention of giving the offending team member a negative reputation, then the teller is using a hidden Dagger. To be nice to someone face to face but muttering a derogatory comment as that person leaves the room is a Dagger response. To be frank, there may be a scary person on your team and you may need to use this style to survive, but do realize that there is an emotional and physical response to holding in all that hidden aggression. Other people will eventually feel uncomfortable with your masked emotions.

The body language of a Dagger responder is conflicted, e.g. a smile and pursed lips. Agreeing with the person while the hand is touching the nose signals that it doesn't really smell right. Saying "I'm listening" while the arms are crossed is another example of this conflicted body language.

Well-practiced Dagger users say something and have their body language generally agree but true feelings are hidden.

Swords, Shields and Daggers are combat-attitude styles. Now we'll discuss the non-combative, peaceful Handshake style.

Handshakes

Handshakes are assertive and cooperative behaviors. They can be compromising or collaborative. With a Handshake response, you communicate that you are important and that the other person is important, too.

Handshakes were originally invented centuries ago to indicate that you held no weapon as you approached someone from another tribe with an extended arm. The right hand was typically extended because it was usually the weapon hand and the left arm was left available so it could protect the heart. In medieval times, knights created the shaking part of the handshake to dislodge any hidden Daggers that might be hidden up the other knight's sleeve. Shaking would last three to five pumps to dislodge the hidden weapons. The message in the Handshake style is "I want to have an honest, open and non-threatening interaction with you."

When you use Handshake responses, you take on a peaceful attitude and let go of your combat mentality. The combat attitude portrays your teammates as the enemy. You may be thinking "I'm not like her" or "I'm the victim and he's the bad guy." As long as you have a combat mentality you don't have to change one iota. You can justify your defensive victim behavior by saying, "I had to yell or keep quiet or tell the team leader because of the way that person treated me." Combat attitude creates an endless cycle of conflict in a team. No matter what the real motive of a team member's behavior, you see it as done intentionally to hurt you. Remember, you have personal power. Claim that power by using the Handshake Responses.

Step five: Understand the real source of the conflict.

Many years ago in one of my first jobs I had an older worker on my team, who was always asking about my personal life, giving me unsolicited advice, and, in my mind, criticizing how I chose to do things. I felt patronized. When I saw her coming down the hall, I said to myself, "Here comes the enemy." I avoided her in the breakroom; I sat at the other end of the table from her at meetings. Although I spent a lot of time complaining about her to my friends, I never spoke to her directly about how I felt. I was great at Armor and Dagger. One day I took on a peaceful Handshake attitude and invited her to lunch. When I asked her about herself and really listened, a miracle happened. I discovered that this woman was the oldest of eleven children and she essentially raised her brothers and sister.

Wow, I thought, she is mothering me! I saw her behavior in a new light. I discovered as we drew closer that she actually admired me and wanted to support me in being a successful speaker. My combat attitude had so successfully obscured my view of her, I hadn't recognized an ally. Our relationship changed not because she changed, but because I changed. The real conflict and the source of that conflict had been inside me.

How many of us look at our teammate's behavior and think,. "If she would just stop _____ (fill in the blank), or if I could just get rid of _____ (fill in the blank), my life would be so much better"? You may be convinced that you just need to change the other person, but being personally powerful is about you changing you. You can't control others' behavior; you can only control yourself, your perception and your response. Stop being the victim of your own heart and mind. True power is not having power over others, but understanding and using the power inside you.

When you are personally powerful, you see yourself much more clearly, both your strengths and your vulnerabilities. Likewise, you see your teammates more clearly as well, both their strengths and vulnerabilities.

There are a number of Handshake responses that you can use to be

personally powerful. These tools include:
- Establishing Commonality (both Verbally and Nonverbally)
- Repeating the Heat
- Requesting More Information
- Ask Why
- Agree
- Apologize
- Express Your Feelings
- Disagree
- Agree to Disagree
- Time Delay

Step six: Utilizing the handshake method.

Establish Commonality

Hey, we like people who are like us, so we like to interact with teammates who are like us. When we meet someone for the first time, we look for commonalities. "You're from Atlanta? Oh, I have an Aunt Bertha who lives there!" That makes us feel safer. At a primal level we are feeling, "I know somebody else from the Atlanta tribe. That person is safe so I guess you're safe, too."

Conflict tends to occur when we emphasize the differences and put the other person in the enemy camp. "I'm not like him — he's got to be right all the time." Or "I don't like her, she is always so pushy." No one wants to cooperate with a team member who is perceived as an enemy.

First, establish some commonality verbally. Find mutual interests such as hobbies, vacation spots, TV shows and music. Or say to yourself, "He thinks the summer project is a priority and so do I." Ask questions such as these out loud: What are our common goals for this project? What do we both see as the quota for this shift? What do we both want to see happen with this client/customer? What result do we both want from this meeting today?

You can also establish commonality nonverbally. When we accentuate the nonverbal differences in our teammates, it also causes conflict. If someone furrows their brow and never smiles, you may see them as a grinch. Guess what — they may see your constantly smiling face and think, "What a space case," or "What a phony," or "He is so slow it takes forever for him to finish a sentence" or "She is so fast she is constantly interrupting me."

When we like a teammate or when we get along with them, we have a tendency to subconsciously match and mirror their body language. They lean forward and you lean forward. They take a sip of soda, you take a sip of soda. They talk in a fast excited voice, you respond in a fast excited voice. They start to use a rapid hand gesture, you start tapping your foot in the same rhythm as their gestures. If you videotaped your conversation and played the tape on fast forward, it would look like you were dancing. You are in sync, and that feels good.

This matching happens naturally, and we rarely notice when someone is in synch with us or vice versa. Only when we or they are out of synch does it show. And that feeling creates conflict.

To establish commonality nonverbally, match the body posture and facial expression of the other person, as well as energy level, gesture, voice, even rate of speech and breathing. Do this slowly and gently while maintaining eye contact. When you match the other person, an interesting thing will happen: you will actually begin to feel what they are feeling. In addition, you communicate to them at the subconscious level thoughts such as, "Hey I get it, I'm with you," or "I'm not your enemy" or " I want to understand you."

Don't mirror aggression. If someone stands over you, legs apart, hands on hips and starts yelling at you, don't jump up and match the behavior. You might get punched. What you can do is subtly come in at a level or two below their energy. Have a little intensity in your voice as you say that you understand the other person is upset. Express your interest or concern as well. Then slowly bring your volume down, slow your rate of speech and relax your body. Your would-be opponent will very likely slow down with you and lower his or her voice as well.

What if a team member is giving you a piece of criticism such as, "Your work stinks and I don't like you"? Then, without using a defensive voice or posture, respond with one or more of the following Handshakes:

Repeat the Heat

Repeat what the criticizer has just said. Repeating the criticism gives the criticizer and you the time to cool down. In addition, repeating the information gives you a better understanding of what the other person has said. The active listening required to paraphrase the comment activates a different portion of your brain than passive listening. Brain researchers say that activation not only helps you understand the information better, but also helps you become calmer. You have heard the advice, "When you get mad count to ten." That works because numbers are processed in the more logical unemotional part of your brain, and counting enables you to switch from the emotional right hemisphere to the unemotional left. Repeating the information can also help you switch to the more rational portion of your brain.

Here's a personal example: when I was working on a project with a rather bossy "always right" team member, he yelled out, "If you would do exactly what I told you to do exactly the way I told you to do it we wouldn't have any problems!" Since this was a team project where we all needed to have equal input, I calmly repeated his statement. Guess what? He had said it so emotionally he hadn't even realized how horrible he sounded. When he heard himself in my repetition, he hung his head and said. "Oh, I'm sorry. That sounded pretty bad." You'll find that repeating can sometimes let the speaker hear themselves, and that is enough to defuse the tension.

Request More Information

"Are you kidding?" you say, "Someone is criticizing me and I'm supposed to ask for more?" Let me clarify: when someone criticizes you and you're not sure what the heck they mean, request more information. If someone says, "I don't like how you're doing your work," calmly ask the person what are their specific complaints. People very often criticize in generalities, especially if they speak emotionally. Emotional statements come from the part of the brain that sees the big picture, not the specific details. By requesting specifics, you get the negative team member to basically switch hemispheres to access the details. You will know that they are very upset if they get flustered or in any way can't give specifics. Their extreme emotions may be overriding their ability to switch hemispheres .

Years ago I was co-authoring my first book with a professor who was known for being a grumbly critic. We had each taken a chapter to work on. I slaved over my chapter for two weeks researching and rewriting it. When we met in his office, he handed me his chapter, and I handed him mine. I got rather nervous as he reached for a red magic marker. He read a few pages and then put a large X across a page. He read a few more pages and put another X. Two X's later, he finished reading, threw the chapter at me and said, "This stinks!" I sat there stunned and then was overcome first with humiliation, then with anger as I thought, what right does he have to be so harsh? Then I thought, I'm so stupid. I'm going to have to work even harder if he doesn't think my ideas and research are any good. I'll have to rewrite the whole thing from scratch.

All of a sudden I realized I was responding defensively. I took a deep breath and in that pause I realized I had no idea what he had meant by "This stinks!" So I asked him, "What about this chapter don't you like?" He replied, "Well, look as this page. There are three spelling errors . . . And here on this page there are two! . . . And look on this page, you have two sentences that don't have parallel construction!" Though he was still upset, I was suddenly happy. All the errors were spelling and grammar. I asked, what about the content? He replied, "Oh that's great, but you have got to do something about your English."

I learned that day that emotions can truly keep you from hearing the real message; asking for specifics really works, and spellcheck doesn't catch all errors.

Requesting more information isn't about catching the criticizer in a generalization. It's about clarifying communication so you know what you can do differently.

Ask Why

Remember when you were little and your mother asked you to do something, you would always ask why? Well, when we get older and someone criticizes us, they are effectively saying do it my way, and we sometimes still need to know why.

Asking why is your right. Perhaps you feel a team member is backing you into a corner and you begin to feel like a victim. Or maybe they are saying stop doing something this way and you don't understand why. Perhaps you don't respond to an e-mail within an hour, and your team member criticizes you. You might ask, "Why is it important for me to check my e-mail every hour?" If their reply is, "Because I look at mine every hour and you should too," you can have a courageous conversation about your schedule and personal preferences. (See my chapter in the book, *Reach For the Stars* for instruction on courageous conversations.) If they say, "Because this project is due at the end of the day, and I can't finish unless you read the document and give me input," then you know their concern has some warrant. You must be sure that your demeanor as you ask why has no hint of judgment or whining but instead indicates a sincere curiosity. The request can be softened by saying, help me understand, or I'm confused, or I want to understand what you mean.

Agree

"What?" you say. " Are you crazy? Agree with a criticism?"

Yep, when the person is right, agree. It's the fastest, most effective way to defuse a negative comment. It works best when you truly do agree. For instance, when you did come late to the meeting, when you didn't help on a project when you should have, or when your mother did dress you funny for work that day.

I like to be right. When I was growing up my father was full bird Colonel in the Air Force and a college professor. He was always right. It was a family ritual when he would make a mistake for him to joke, "First mistake I ever made." Years later when I went out into the world and started my business I felt I was always right. That it was part of my genetic heritage. Well, always being right means that everybody else in the room is always wrong. Pretty soon nobody wants to be in the room with you.

Then I started teaching the Handshake nondefensive options. One day, as I was riding in a car with a team member, he said something, and I told him he was wrong. He turned to me and gave me the evidence to prove he was right. I said, "Oh you're right! I was wrong." There was a potent silence, the earth moved. The planets realigned. I felt a strange peace come over me. My team member's jaw dropped, and he said, "Do you realize that in all the time we've worked together that's the very first time you let me be right?" I quickly replied, "No, you're wrong!" He started laughing, and I realized that I had tried to make him wrong again.

Agreeing takes away the negative comment's power. There is nothing more your teammate can say. Though I still like to be right, I have found, as you will, that there is a release and an ease that comes with agreeing.

Apologize

You've done something wrong and instead of excusing yourself out of it, just say a short and simple "I'm sorry." Or "I'm sorry I messed up." It seems so easy to say, "It's not my fault." "It's so and so on the team's fault." Or, "I got it late or I would have gotten it to you on time." We think of these as explanations or justifications, but they are really defensive Shields.

Express What You Are Feeling

"What do mean tell them how I'm feeling?" you may wonder. "You mean tell them how miffed I am?"

Nope. Tell them they said something upsetting to you. Not, "You make me mad." But, "When you say that I don't care about our project, I get upset." Notice that you don't say "you make me mad" and that you also repeat the criticism. Why do you need to tell them your emotional response to their statement? Because some people have no idea how their negative comments affect others. They can't or won't think about it. The people who have difficulty understanding are usually using the logical left hemisphere, sometimes called the critique brain. This makes the person great at telling you what specifically is wrong or what they don't like, but without the input of the right brain where emotions are considered. They don't think about how their criticism may effect you. For these people you need to clue them in. Again, don't place blame by saying, "You make me angry." The truth is you choose to be angry, they don't make you angry. Also angry and mad are emotion laden words.

Upset, disturbed, unhappy and other words besides angry and mad are usually more effective.

Disagree

Disagreeing isn't about making the other person wrong. It's about letting them feel however they want to feel and you getting to feel whatever you want. The first step in disagreeing is to listen carefully to what the team member has said and then Repeat the Heat, so they have no doubt that you heard them, then you disagree. For example: "You feel . . . I disagree, I feel . . ."

Notice the first step is not, "You're wrong, and your mother wears army boots."

If you say to a team member, you're wrong, that person is going to turn around and say, "No, you're wrong." This back and forth attacking doesn't solve a thing. Simply repeat what they have said. Then disagree. If that doesn't diffuse it and they keep trying to convince you that they are right and you are wrong, try the next response.

Agree to Disagree

In this response you both are adamant in your opinions, and neither is going to change the other's mind.

I was working on a project with a team member and one issue came up that we just kept disagreeing on. I finally said, "It's important to me that we get along on this project. I can tell you that I feel strongly on this issue and you're not going to say anything to change my mind, so why don't we agree to disagree? I'll respect your opinion and you respect mine, and if it comes up in a team meeting we will just smile knowingly at each other." He actually laughed and said okay!

Delay It

"Oh, boy, you mean I can stuff it or put it off for another meeting?"

Nope. A delay is not a Shield technique. No stuffing allowed. It's also not a Dagger technique. No saving it for ammunition later. Time delay is more like a time out. It can be as short and simple as saying,. "Let me think about it before I respond." You might just take a deep breath or say, "Let's go get a cup of coffee or coke and come back and talk about this." It's just a brief break to let any intense negative emotions dissipate. However, after a delay of 24 hours, your brain will only hold onto your side of the discussion. The more time that passes the more right you become and the more wrong the other person is. So just ask for or suggest a short break.

For example, "This is important to me, but the emotions are pretty intense. I think we could work this out if we took a break and came back after lunch and talked about it." Notice the wording. You don't say, "You're too mad now to be reasonable. I need you to calm down." Make the emotions separate from them or take ownership of yours. You might say, "I'm too emotional to solve this right now. Can we take a break here and talk about it." Or "I'm overwhelmed with a project now, and this is important to me. Can we talk about it at 3:00 after I'm done and I can give it the attention it deserves?" Notice that you are making an appointment to deal with the issue.

Integrating the Handshake Tools

Now you have enough Handshake tools to make a choice in responding. As you start practicing them, you will probably find one that seems to be more comfortable. Use that tool till it becomes second nature and you don't have to think about it or hesitate. In the meantime take the quick reference sheet of Handshake options given below and tape them somewhere. Maybe pin it to your cubicle wall or workstation. Or incorporate them into your screen saver or the first page of your Daytimer. Put them somewhere you'll be reminded to use them. Don't let them be a mere bookmark. Let them help you change the way you deal with conflict.

Little by little these Handshake options have helped me. They were awkward at first and I still have my favorites. I knew they were really a part of me about a year after I started using them. I was doing a workshop for the elders of a church in Richmond, Virginia. I had just taught the Handshake options and given the class a break. One of the elders of the church came up during the break and said, "These options are bull . . ." I replied, "Oh, what about them don't you like?" He looked at me funny and said, "Darn it, we decided at the beginning of break that we would all criticize you and get you defensive and that Handshakes wouldn't work, but you didn't hesitate. You really were curious. You didn't get mad at all."

I realized in that moment that I hadn't felt defensive and that by using the tools over and over I was more in control of myself. I had power in conflict.

These responses can make a difference in your life. You just need to practice them. Be aware that in every conflict you have choices. As you work with your team, you can put away your Swords, Shields and Daggers. You now have personal power.

Handshake Options Reference Sheet

Listen to your team member and acknowledge him or her. Then use one or more of these options:

Establish Commonality Verbally — Look for what you agree on rather than differences.

Establish Commonality Nonverbally — Match the other person's body language, energy level and breathing while maintaining eye contact.

Repeat the Heat — In a calm voice repeat what the criticizer has just said.

Request More Information — Ask for the details or a specific example of the offending behavior.

Ask Why — Use your right to discover the consequences of your behavior.

Agree — If the statement is true, agree with it. Acknowledge that the other person is right.

Apologize — Heal the mistake, and don't add a justification or an excuse.

Express Your Feelings — If the other person is clueless and not "out to get you," let them know how their comments or criticisms made you feel.

Disagree — Repeat what the other person said, then disagree. You can have your own opinion without making the other person wrong.

Agree to Disagree — Make an agreement to disagree and move on to other things.

Time Delay — Make an appointment to deal with the issues later if there is too much emotion.

ABOUT PATTI WOOD, M.A., CSP

P atti Wood is an international speaker, trainer and author. Since 1982 she has designed and led keynotes, workshops and convention seminars for organizations such as AT&T, Chick-fil-A, Colgate-Palmolive, Citicorp, Hewlett Packard, GTE, Nortel, Old Navy, and the U.S. Army. She delivers over 100 presentations a year, and 75% of her business is from clients asking her back. Clients describe her as dynamic, high-energy and a powerhouse presenter. Patti develops a warm, laughter-filled relationship with her audience that leaves participants talking in the halls about what they've learned.

Patti has been interviewed on radio and television as an expert on body language. Time *magazine recognized her non-verbal communication course at Florida State University as one of the top in the nation.*

Contact Information:
Patti Wood
Communication Dynamics
2343 Hunting Valley Drive
Decatur, GA 30033

Phone: (404) 315-7397
Fax: (404) 315-9255
E-mail: PattiWood@mindspring.com
Web: www.PattiWood.net

THE PATHWAY TO SUCCESS

by Juanita Sanders Cribb

Take Control of Your Life

It's been said, life is full of instructions. Some lessons are mastered immediately. Others are only partially revealed, so it seems that mastery of an assignment or completing the instructions is impossible. Then you realize that the gradual exposure of content is deliberate. In life we may never master lessons, but we can understand enough to play by the rules.

The rules are not complex, just ever changing. We are all aware of the saying, "By the time I learned all the rules, they changed the game." Life catches us off guard or disappoints us, when in reality, we should buckle up and be prepared for the whirlwind changes of life. In fact, that is the only rule we can depend on. Life brings rules and the rules are constantly changing. So how does one prepare for the changes of life?

We prepare by learning a few basic rules and working those rules to mastery. Some rules become foundational and applicable to every occurrence in life. These I learned early in life, lessons called *motivation, determination, persistence, and drive!*

If we are to succeed, taking *control* is imperative. One highlight in life is when we become old enough to get a driver's license. It is a sign of accomplishment, responsibility and mastery! We learn all the rules of driving and then we practice for at least a year using a learner's permit. We spend a year in anticipation and a year of practice just to learn to *take control* and *drive.*

Driving gives freedom and flexibility. The young driver is free to set his or her own schedule, and the parents have added flexibility for work and other tasks. One person deciding to *take control* impacts all!

When do we realize that we are prepared to take control? When we become motivated enough to overcome any and every obstacle. This persistent desire will cause you to become determined and fuel your motivation. The word motivation has a root structure — *mo.* This part of the word is also associated with words such as motive and motion. All relate to an action, desire, process of changing, and, quite simply, movement. Webster defines motivation as "moved to action."

If we want a higher station in life, we must be willing to move to action. This action requires an internal plus an external motivator. I like to think of it as a mechanism within us. It's like a motor. It requires a spark from a small plug. Once we ignite this plug, it cranks up the engine and can move a two-ton vehicle. Isn't that amazing? Just a spark! We can spark and entice our minds to create a new plan of action; however, if we do not physically move our bodies, nothing happens. It's been said that insanity is doing the same thing in the same way expecting a different outcome.

Our lives are programmed from birth. We record all experiences. Those experiences become our reality and our truth. These beliefs become our guiding forces and patterns. To reprogram and set our minds to a higher level of creativity, we must begin by releasing old habits created out of years of self-limiting behavior.

Releasing negative feelings from the past will give you the drive to pursue and, ultimately, achieve your goals. It's like having a car with the brakes on. It might inch along but not smoothly. Eventually the brakes will wear out. A life held in bondage by old feelings and events is a life of torture. Let go! You need drive to attain your desires for today and tomorrow. Olympic gold medal winners like Jackie Joyner Kersey break world records because of that unstoppable force known as drive. Business legends like cosmetics queen Mary Kay Ashe are as noted for their drive as they are for their success.

An important element of every rag-to-riches story is drive. Drive gives you energy for surmounting the toughest roadblocks on your path to success. Drive gets you unstuck. Without a driving surge of emotional and physical energy, it's impossible to overcome the obstacles that will, inevitably, crop up on the road to success. In the world of motivation we promote the idea of "speaking with power, feeling and conviction." We believe this is a panacea to many ills. This might sound simple, yet most answers to our greatest challenges in life are simple. We condition ourselves to believe what is said to us and around us.

We continue these patterns by speaking feelings of doubt to ourselves and to others. Words like, "I don't really think they want me for that job." Or words like, "I knew he or she would get the promotion because . . ." It really does not matter what the "because" is. The only thing that matters is that others have convinced you, and you are convincing yourself.

I like to call this the Scarcity and Shortage Mode. In this pattern of thinking, we generally talk ourselves out of taking positive action and forward steps. This mode of thinking is created out of emotions, not reality. When we operate from a feeling, an emotion, it does not yield us to a level playing field. The field of emotion is full of ditches. This is not a safe place. Emotion is unstable and unsettling. Emotions distort reality and can cause us to miss many opportunities for health, wealth and happiness.

Scarcity and Shortage operate either from a conscience-stricken or ashamed outlook.

We hide or disown our past failures and shortcomings. Learning to talk to ourselves positively and by taking persistent baby steps forward, we find our greatest and best selves. How did this negative self-talk begin? From our birth, adults are constantly talking to us. From the beginning it's instructions about how to become more of a human being. As time passes, we experience the opinions of adults from parents to teachers whose assessments usually have a deep and lasting impact on our lives, even throughout adulthood. The attitude which we use when facing daily challenges relates to our recent perception but more to the programming from a long time ago. We learn by what we do and by what we hear. For example, many relationships are based upon what our fathers and mothers experienced and passed on to us. Whether we think that men are "dogs" or that women are "moochers" is based on prior conversations more than recent realities. Distorting current experiences with past conversations is very easy. In fact, we find in life that we get very little of what we "want" but more of what we "expect." Interesting, since most of us would bet the farm that we "want" more than we get. The only way to get more, is to expect more.

Remember the saying, "It's okay if you talk to yourself if you don't answer"? Well, I disagree. If we accept that we have more than 50,000 thoughts per day, we are talking to ourselves whether we want to or not. So why not take advantage of this automatic physical function and begin to reprogram that inner conversation.

Saying a thing loudly and often enough causes you not only to hear yourself but hopefully believe in yourself. Without belief, having a life of meaning and purpose is impossible. Belief becomes the fuel of drive. You can only move toward something that you believe is possible for you.

It takes only one thought to change your life. Isn't that what happened with the pet rock idea and the tennis shoe revolution? Ideas that were not genius, just acted upon. Part of success is the ability to sell yourself on your own ideas.

Sales ability begins with thinking that something is valuable. Every day of our lives we are selling ourselves or someone else on the idea of possibilities. What is keeping your idea from coming forth energetically and positively? Well, it could be because 80 percent of your

50,000 thoughts are *negative*.

That's right, negative. We talk ourselves down and we discourage others. For example, we say "I doubt that," or "How will you do that?" Most of the time when we get a good idea, the how, why and belief will build over time. We do not need constant reminders from the outside that the task is a major undertaking; usually, we have enough doubt for ourselves.

So it becomes very important to talk to yourself about possibilities. These possibilities and beliefs will fuel your greatest desires. Persist! Did some unpleasant experience from the past force you to become a winner? Stories of triumph and courage are shown to us every day. It's not the struggle but drive and determination that complete the task. Some say just don't give up. If only life were that simple; of course, don't give up. However, we must learn to continue to get up every time we are knocked down. They call this perseverance. We must create a pattern of surviving the harshest tests of life, whether that is talking to yourself, meditating, exercising for stress relief, seeking professional counseling, or simply crying for release. If you complete the cycle of pain, you can begin to recreate another opportunity for success. So, bless your negative past before you release it forever to its final resting place. Learn the lessons you can, and store the others for the future. Take control of your life and allow ideas to fuel your motivation. Use your past as a stepping stone, not a stumbling block, to a better you.

Forgiveness Equals Freedom

Les Brown was the catalyst of this awareness for me. He always said, as I murmured about certain challenges I was facing, "Nitaboo, you handle it with grace or it will forever be in your face." That was quite an interesting notion. At that time I did not realize certain people and circumstances were holding me back because of the emotion I harbored toward them.

The scriptures often relate to God's grace and mercy toward us.

How then could I expect from others what I was unwilling to give. Another spiritual law says we get what we give out. It is the law of reaping and sowing, and in universal law it is the law of karma. On the street it's simply what goes around, comes around. So this idea is nothing to take lightly. How many people do you know still carrying around horror stories of loves lost, relationships betrayed, promotions denied, jobs lost due to a layoff or firing and oh yeah, the big one, death? The list goes on and on. Handle it with grace (*forgive*) or it will stay in your face.

I know what it's like to lose a job, have a boyfriend stolen, get cheated out of a business deal, have an unfaithful friend, experience rejection, feel unappreciated and unloved, and the anguishing pain of losing a loved one to death. Believe me: Every human being at some time or another will have some type of character-building experience. How do you make it? Forgive! It sounds simple and it is. Some of you might ask, how does forgiveness relate to death?

Well, if you haven't been there, you won't understand how angry with God and everyone else you can become. When my mother died, I deliberately avoided my women friends whose mothers were alive, especially if they had a good relationship like my mom and me. I couldn't tolerate those that were unappreciative of having a mom. Yes, some mothers are cantankerous, noisy and meddlesome; they are still a joy. When you realize that some people never experience that kind of nurturing relationship, forgiveness can become a critical enhancement to your life.

Have you ever taken a long trip or vacation? Packing can be quite challenging. Is the weather warm or cold? There's always a chance of rain. You will need dressy clothes and some casual outfits. Shoes, dressy and casual. Toiletries, and heaven forbid if it's winter and we have to lug a coat around. Packing takes time. Oops, they canceled the trip! Though you are prepared, what do you do now? Do you take those bags with you everywhere you go, telling everyone about the opportunity missed and all the time it took to prepare to go? So you decide to keep those bags packed. You tell everyone you encounter about your canceled trip, and carry those bags with you as reminders everywhere you go. Is this ridiculous? No more ridiculous than the emotional baggage we hold onto most, if not all, of our lives.

Let go! Eighty percent of the people you meet don't care, and the other twenty percent are glad it's you and not them. So think about it: *nobody really cares!*

Forgiveness is an emotional, psychological, and spiritual healing process that frees you. Without forgiveness, you become a perpetual victim. Forgiveness allows you to enjoy the present and to plan for the future. Forgiving someone else is much more important for you than it is for the person who hurt you.

Forgiving operates as emotional cleaning, uncluttering your mind to pursue new goals, richer experiences, and warmer relationships. Forgiveness is a force that empowers victims to transform themselves into victors. You can forgive anyone for anything.

Begin to begin the healing force of forgiveness by acknowledging that today things are different. Reflect on experiences with objectivity. Ask valid questions of yourself. What was my role? What is the lesson learned? How will I avoid this next time? Is it foolish to experience the same thing repeatedly? So with that in mind, is it them or is it you?

Dwelling on past memories and experiences can sabotage your life. Memories, conscious or not, of betrayal and deceptions in families, friendships and romantic relationships can prevent you from opening up to close relationships, personal and professional growth — and their rewards — today. Rewrite the foundation and rework the future.

Today

Today, I plant a seed called forgiveness.
My greatest potential is yet to be revealed.
My greatest wisdom is yet to be realized.
A seed. Strength, wisdom, solutions, ideas.
Life's quandaries are yet to be resolved.
For today, I planted a seed.

— Juanita Sanders Cribb

ABOUT JUANITA SANDERS CRIBB

J uanita Cribb has been called one of "America's best and brightest business professionals," by Dollars and Sense Magazine. *Her insightful and savvy approach to developing successful employees and careers will propel you to new heights as you carve the path to success in your field. A professional trainer, motivational speaker and public servant, Juanita's refreshing style remains in constant demand, particularly for political, religious and educational institutions across North America as she delivers The Pathway to Success.*

Contact Information:
Juanita Cribb
Crystal Communications Corporation
P.O. Box 43027
Atlanta, GA 30336-0027

Phone: (770) 469-4247
Fax: (770) 413-9534
E-mail: CCCorp98@aol.com
Web: www.JuanitaCribb.com

Your Team Members Don't Have to Be Perfect

by Mike Marino, Jr.

In Person

I would like to say that *the biggest room in the world is the room for improvement.* I believe everyone wants to constantly improve. I believe each one of us is created as *perfection*; however, the results we create are excellent, so there is lots of room for improvement in what we do. The associates I hired in my bicycle and lawnmower shop were never perfect; however, they were excellent. Working with them as they improved taught me new ways to show forgiveness, understanding, and patience.

My first employee was in a wheelchair from an auto accident that happened when he was sixteen. I hired him to answer the telephone and talk to customers who came into the store. My second employee had one arm. Word spread that I hired people with physical challenges. The placement officer at a local community college with a rehabilitation school called on my business about hiring people with physical and mental disabilities.

One day the placement officer asked me to interview a young man who was having trouble finding a job. He told me that David was a little shy, did not talk much and was afraid to go on interviews. He requested that I grant David an interview just for practice. He plainly told David that I had no positions open at the time and the interview was just for practice.

When David came in for the interview, he hardly said a word. I told him what we do at the bicycle shop and showed him around. When the interview was over I told him I would keep his application on file. Then I took a few minutes to coach David on how to apply for a job. I told David to keep showing up (figuratively) because the number one thing an employer wants in an associate is dependability.

David was very quiet (he was evaluated as a slow learner in school). Every ten days or so, for weeks after the interview, David walked into the bicycle shop and stood by the front door. He never said a word, just stood by the door. I would tell him kindly, "I really do not have any positions open at this time." I wished he would go away, but he kept showing up!

The shop was a very labor-intensive place to work, with students unloading trucks, assembling bicycles and lawnmowers, making repairs and waiting on customers. I usually had seventeen employees at one time, mostly high school and college students. David continued to keep coming by about every ten days. He never said a word.

One day, shortly before Christmas, a large tractor-trailer backed up to the shop, packed with 250 new, unassembled bicycles. It had to be unloaded right away or the driver would leave, and it might be a long time before I could get him back for the delivery. It was raining. Some of my student workers (without physical limitations) chose not to brave the weather to get into work, so I was short handed. The place was crowded with shoppers. Frustrated customers were waiting to be served. A line formed at the counter. It seemed everything was going wrong and on top of it, David came in the front door and just stood there. I looked at him and barked, "Well, all right! Fill out a time card and help me unload this truck!"

David worked for my bicycle shop for eighteen years. His dedication was a model for me. He came to work every day thirty minutes early. He could talk; however, he rarely chose to. He was a man of few words. He drove my truck and made deliveries. He went to the bank to make daily deposits. David would assemble and check out all of the new lawnmowers. The customers would brag about David, saying, "He doesn't talk, but he really shows you how to operate a lawnmower!" I got into the habit of looking over at David for advice when I was making decisions. David would nod or shake his head. He helped me make a lot of good choices. Eventually, I let David run the business when I was out of the store taking care of other business.

David was a blessing. I really feel that God sent David to me. I did my best to find David a better paying job with better benefits. However, he would not leave! I learned much from him.

David drove a Corvette. One day a college student employee said, "Mr. Mike, you must be paying David more money than you do us, look at what he is driving." Within earshot, David heard. He simply held up his lunch bag, implying, "I bring my lunch. You buy your lunch. It is not how much you earn, it's how you manage your earning."

I am so glad that David kept showing up. He was my last employee when I retired and closed the shop.

I was able to hire over eighty-five women and men with physical and mental challenges and coach them into more gainful employment in the community. I would look for what they could do, not what they could not do, as it is easy to find what people cannot do. I was 98 percent successful. I had just a few results that did not work out. I found my associates to be loyal, honest, and dependable. Consciously, I worked to remove their fear of being fired by encouraging them to make business decisions freely and by not pouncing on their mistakes.

I encouraged my employees to constantly look to better themselves, whether it was within my company or somewhere else. I loved to coach them on how to apply for jobs and encouraged them to tell their prospective employers, "Please do not look at my disability. Look at my ability. Let me show you what I can do. I am honest, I am dependable, and I am willing to listen and learn." I told my associates if they left me for a better job and it did not work out, they could always come back. I looked for better paying jobs for my employees so I could hire more people with limitations who needed a place to enter the job market. I was blessed beyond my fondest dreams when I hired people with physical and mental challenges. Listening to and learning from them was a bountiful gift sent to me.

Only thoughts can limit people. *Ordinary people can do extraordinary things.* Your team members are not perfect and that's okay. They can still do excellent things.

When I graduated from school, I was connected with a group of thirty people that made a pact to stick together for life. One particular girl is the leader. She has kept us all together for years with a newsletter that announces weddings, births, engagements and deaths (three so far). As years go by, the twenty-seven remaining are scattered around the world. Our leader arranges community projects each month for all of us to participate in, no matter where we are located. Our pact is to "hit and run" — we do good without getting credit, which is the whole idea. Knowing that no one knows makes us feel good. It helps me to walk around with a smile most of the time. We have a secret.

One day I answered the phone at my bicycle shop and our leader was on the phone. She said that I was to be in Lafayette, Louisiana, that Sunday for a community project. We were to entertain forty abused children. I was to bring potato chips and soft drinks. The girls would decorate the children's faces, and we would give them gifts and play games. The event was at an oil field playground at noon. The members of the group of twenty-seven that were out of town or out of the country had to call a pay phone at the shelter on the playground at a certain time of the day. Everyone had to participate in some way — no matter what time it was where he or she was calling from. Everyone was expected to participate.

When I hung up the phone, I called Tony, who worked for me answering the phones at my store. He had been in an auto accident when he was sixteen and was now confined to a wheel chair. He did not go out much and I thought it would be good for him. He was so happy I called, and his mother said that she would have him ready for nine o'clock on Sunday morning.

When I hung up the phone, Kenny, one of my cashiers, asked if he could go with us. I told him not to listen in on my phone conversations anymore! Then I said, "Okay, but you must be in front of the bicycle shop on Sunday morning at ten o'clock because it takes two hours to get to Lafayette from New Orleans." Born with cerebral palsy, Kenny relied on crutches to walk.

That Sunday morning, I said good-bye to my understanding wife and I picked up Tony. As I drove up to the shop for Kenny, I saw he was with a young man who was also using crutches for support.

Kenny said, "This is my friend Richard. I knew you wouldn't mind if he came along. He does not get out much." I helped the men get into the back seat of my Ford van, set their crutches on top of Tony's folded wheelchair in the back, and we were off to Lafayette.

Tony, Kenny and I talked all the way to Lafayette. Richard said very little. At the playground, we fixed hot dogs for the children. The girls painted faces and we gave out presents. The music was wonderful. As we say in Louisiana, "We passed a good time."

On the trip back home, it was starting to get dark as we approached Baton Rouge. Everyone got quiet and rode in silence. I could hear the tires on the road and every once in awhile I could hear Tony, sitting next to me, sigh under his breath, "Oh me." The silence was creepy.

Coming from a family of ten children, I got used to noise. Stationed on an attack aircraft carrier with a bunk directly under the catapult machinery that fired the jets off the ship, I got comfortable with noise. To disrupt the quiet, I said, "Let's play life boat. This van is a big pleasure boat. A friend of mine lent me his boat for the weekend and I decided to take you guys boating. We cruised out of the marina in Lake Pontchartrain and headed into the open waters of the Gulf of Mexico. We are now far from land. The radio is not working. The boat hit some sunken oil equipment, tearing a big hole, and now the boat is taking on water. There is only one life preserver on board. It will hold only one person. The boat is going down. We are in very deep water. Everyone will get sixty seconds to say why he should get the one life preserver, *why he should live.*

"Since I am responsible for the boat, I will get to go first. My name is Mike Marino. I have a wife and two children and I have five brothers and four sisters who need me. My parents need me." I started saying things that I had accomplished in my life and that I deserved to live because I wanted to continue serving other people and trying to make a difference in the world. At the end of my one minute, I said, "I vote for me getting the life preserver." Then I added, "Tony, it's now your turn."

Tony, 29, had been in an auto accident when he was sixteen, drag racing with other teenagers. He had been in the back seat. The accident left him in a coma for three months. I met him in Children's Hospital when I was doing volunteer work. From the time I hired him, I would often go by his house to give him a ride to my bicycle shop, where he answered the phone through a head set.

Tony said, "I vote for you, too." I said, "Tony you have fifty-five more seconds to say something good about yourself! The boat is sinking, everyone is going to die except the one with the life preserver!"Tony replied, "I still vote for you."

Now it was Kenny's turn. He was born with serious cerebral palsy; however, it did not affect his speech. Kenny's mother died of a brain tumor. The oldest of four sons, he helped raise his younger brothers. Kenny, very smart, was my cashier and did all of the warranty paper work for the business. From the back seat Kenny said, "I vote for you, too, because I believe that if you live, you will find a way to come back and save us." I said, "No, you cannot change the rules, everyone dies, except the one that gets the most votes. You have thirty more seconds to vote for yourself Kenny." "No, I vote for you," he said again.

Now it was Richard's turn to vote. Richard, in his middle thirties with a thick shock of hair like a young Elvis, also had cerebral palsy. His speech was much impaired and he spoke very slowly; still it was hard to understand him. He started out, "I know that I cannot do much because of my handicap; however, I am very good on the computer. I type eleven words a minute with the eraser of a pencil. I do not want to die out here in the Gulf of Mexico. My mother, that I live with, and my brother would be very sad. Mother needs me. My brother has a little boy, five-months-old, and I have a relationship with him. I want to live to see him grow up. If someone would give me a chance, I could work and do good for someone. Nobody will give me a chance. I want to vote for myself."

One second of silence passed and Tony and Kenny asked together at the same time. "Can we vote again?"

I said, "No! Sometimes in life you get only one chance to vote for yourself. You may get rushed to the hospital for open-heart surgery and you may have to sign a paper to allow the surgeons to operate. You cannot say, "I'm scared. Let's wait.' If you wait you may need a heart transplant instead of just repair. You must always be ready to vote for yourself. Since I am the captain of the boat, I have the right to give my vote away if I want to. I gave my vote to Richard for voting for himself."And with that I prayed that Tony and Kenny better appreciate the value of voting for themselves.

I knew my accountant would be a little upset because he was always after me for having too many employees, but I couldn't help myself. I hired Richard. He did my bookkeeping. He did all the accounts receivable, accounts payable and payroll. He typed holding a pencil upside down with the eraser pressing the keys. He worked hard. When I became a motivational speaker, Richard attended many of my speeches.

After two years he was proud to tell me he had applied for a job in payroll with the U.S. Department of Agriculture's Finance Center. They hired him on a trial basis, but on his second day he discovered a major error in their payroll system so they rewarded him with a permanent job. He has since had several promotions and has stopped by to show me his new car.

If you ever saw Richard walking down the street on his crutches, you would think it was impossible for him to drive a car, but he has learned how. When people ask Richard how he does all that he does, he replies, "If you don't vote for yourself, nobody votes for you."

I have had the privilege to work and play with excellent, not perfect, people. A long time ago I discovered something about David, Tony, Kenny, Richard, and all of the other men and women I have employed as associates: I was not sent to help them grow, they were sent to help me grow. I don't mean growing my business, I mean growing intellectually and emotionally. Working with them as they improved their skills and sharply raised their self-value taught me new ways to show forgiveness, understanding, and patience.

The following are *20 Rules to Make Life More Fun*. Most are daily, some weekly or monthly. These help me be a contributing member of my teams: family, profession and community.

1. Stay very close to your heart! Never change who you are. Stay true to your style of learning.
2. Daily, tell three people how you really feel. Ask three people for what you really want.
3. Be committed to yourself, your family, and your profession.
4. Follow your own instructions. (You're the authority in your life.)
5. Call a buddy.
6. Attend a weekly group meeting.
7. Have Fun!
8. Never disclose anyone else's experience. (Don't gossip)
9. Complete one community project each month.
10. Be honest. Come from integrity.
11. Write in your log daily.
12. Get it off your chest as soon as possible.
13. Do not accept limitations — others, or your own.
14. Know where your notebook is at all times.
15. Go dancing and have Fun!
16. Complete your goals.
17. Schedule a 60-day plan. Have something to look forward to in your future.
18. Review your goals and these ground rules daily.
19. Invite other people into your life. Success is a team effort. Don't be the Lone Ranger.

20. Don't give away your power. Say "yes" when you want to say "yes" and "no" when you want to say "no."

ABOUT MIKE MARINO, JR.

*M*ike Marino calls himself a Resource Awareness Coach on Human *Potential. He writes and speaks on fun as a resource for pleasure, productivity and maximizing potential. For 28 years Mike owned a retail store in New Orleans, where he hired 85 handicapped men and women through Delgado College's rehabilitation program, taught them life-changing business skills and coached them to explore their potentials. Additionally he hired dozens of students, which enabled them to pay their way through college and gain hands-on experience of vital career-building skills, such as taking responsibility and enjoying their work. For the past 14 years, Mike has taught Applied Economics for the Junior Achievement program.*

Mike is a member of the American Society for Training and Development and Toastmasters International. He is the grandfather of 4, father of 2 and husband of 1. He believes that wherever you are in life, you could be having more fun on the dance floor of life!

Contact Information:
Mike Marino, Jr.
In Person
P.O. Box 9015
Metairie, LA 70055

Phone: (504) 833-4405
E-mail: InPerson@gs.net
Web: www.tfrick.com/Marino

WHEN DID WE QUIT HOLDING HANDS?

by Phyllis May, Ph.D.

Teamwork. The key to success!!! How can that be when we Americans have been brought up to value self-reliance and individualism? Competitiveness is instilled as a virtue that is a key to success. Where or how can teamwork fit into this model?

A troop of Boy Scouts gathered for their annual hike in the woods. Taking off at sunrise, they began a fifteen-mile trek through some of the most scenic grounds in the country. About midmorning, the Scouts came across an abandoned section of railroad track. Each, in turn, tried to walk the narrow rails, but after only a few unsteady steps, each lost his balance and tumbled off.

Two of the Scouts, after watching one after another fall off the iron rail, offered a bet to the rest of the troop. The two bet that they could both walk the entire length of the railroad track without falling off even once.

The other boys laughed and said, "No way!" Challenged to make good their boast, the two boys jumped up on opposite rails, simply reached out and held hands to balance each other, and steadily walked the entire section of track with no difficulty.

How easy it was, simply by working together as a team. When people help each other, freely and voluntarily, there is a spirit of teamwork that can conquer a multitude of problems. When we don't cooperate, the whole system can fall apart. Reach out to your team-

mates and never quit holding hands.

Most of us grew up learning about teams only as they related to athletics. It probably wasn't until we got into a work environment, where the possibility of transferring the positive aspects of teams, took on new meaning with endless possibilities. Successful athletic teams have learned that although each team member may come from a variety of backgrounds, with a wide range of skills or talents and often little in terms of personal commonalities — their focus on a common goal gives them the bond needed to strive for team success. However, that team success has to be learned.

It is important to realize that team success doesn't just happen. It isn't accidental or luck. It is developed and individual team members who understand team dynamics and the evolution of a successful team will be instrumental in its ultimate success. Seldom is a team successful unless the spirit is positive and invigorating.

At a time when leadership models are changing, those used to command leadership recognize more readily the value of synergy (collective energy), empowerment, collegiality and the power of a common interest.

A broad definition of a team is two or more persons who must coordinate with each other in order to get some job done. These two or more people need not have anything in common — other than a mutual goal. Therefore, teams may not always be called teams. These theories apply to committees, boards of directors, school boards or committees and political "teams" such as councils and commissions. Two or more people with a common goal, regardless of what they are called, are a team.

In the case of some of the previous group examples, it is possible that in groups such as these that were not formed specifically as teams, there are times when they function as a team and times when they do not. When they are not functioning with a common goal, they are simply a group.

In reality, because team members do not have to be as homogenous as is necessary in many groups, team spirit is a major element of success. Often with such a conglomeration of personalities, the effectiveness needed might not be achieved without an understanding of the group dynamics.

To begin with, it helps if team members have some choice about participating in as well as belonging to the team. Being forced to be a team member often means that the participation level is minimal. Or, being assigned to a team without input can be just as negative.

When the team is formed or membership changes, a process for team growth must take place. First, there is leadership within the group. Oftentimes, as in a board of directors, there is a process for selecting the leadership team. Other, more informal, groups select their leaders in a variety of ways. Without a process for selecting a leader, usually one will emerge from the group. But there must be an identified leader to guide, motivate and "coach" the members.

While it takes time, serious groups would benefit from taking the time early on to administer some type of personality assessment. There are several different choices available, and doing this in a group setting provides a better understanding of individual team and board members in the group. This exercise can serve as an icebreaker if it is a newly formed group. And, having a better understanding of the personality traits of team members is advantageous as time goes on. A great deal of insight can be gained which will help, especially if there are challenging endeavors ahead or if there are some personality clashes which could interfere with the successful functioning of the team.

Whether your team is a more formal/official group operating with an agenda or one operating in an informal setting, guidelines should be established early. If the group determines these, the chances are greater that these will be respected — which will keep the group on task.

Encouraging the group to identify their common bond, which should be the ultimate goal, provides the focus. Determining the process for achieving the success of the team is most effective when the members have input and, therefore, buy-in.

Unless it is a formal or official group, using consensus as opposed to voting provides more opportunity for acceptance of ideas, perhaps in a modification of an original proposal. Therefore, this is another important step which encourages positive team spirit.

Effective teams encourage a sense of community. This means that all of these individuals working together share a commitment to understand and honor differing perceptions and concerns in an environment of trust. Trust and respect are absolute essentials to the success of any effective team. Few things are as essential for morale (and that morale helps generate the necessary positive team spirit).

It is assumed that effective teams are obviously composed of effective team members. Philip Grant, a professor of management at Husson College in Bangor, Maine, has identified a list of attributes which a good team player possesses. These characteristics include:

• *Liking, trusting and respecting each other.* The most effective teamwork takes place when team members feel positively toward one another, value other members' views, and know they can depend on one another. In such an atmosphere, members put a lot of effort into resolving problems and promoting team success. But there is no reason to believe a group of people will like, trust, and respect one another automatically, just because you tell them they're now a team. Grant recommends training in interpersonal skills (perhaps including some sensitivity training) to help the process along.

• *Supporting and helping others.* High-performance team players are willing to go beyond the boundaries of their own tasks and successes. They not only help others when asked but provide assistance on their own initiative. They share information freely instead of hoarding it for their own advancement. They provide emotional support to other team members, praise their efforts, and take action to relieve others' pressures and frustrations. They are concerned about the morale and performance of the entire group.

• *Understanding and appreciating others' roles.* If each appreciates the different activities and goals of his fellows, Grant says, "Team members can better coordinate their efforts with the efforts of others." They build on one another's contributions instead of duplicating or interfering with them. And they adjust their own work schedules (deadlines for particular pieces of a larger project, etc.) to avoid placing unreasonable demands on others.

• *Communicating effectively.* Successful team members listen empathetically, ignore distractions, respond without defensiveness to constructive criticism, and don't allow their biases to color the messages they send or receive. They ask questions when they don't understand something and provide feedback to other team members. They keep direct, two-way communication lines open between themselves and others. They use whatever means of communication are appropriate for a given situation and are conscious of possible communication barriers, be they semantic, perceptual, or physical.

• *Openly confronting problems and knowing how to resolve conflict.* The team environment is interdependent. One person's unresolved problem can quickly snowball, interfering with group progress. Good team members, Grant says, promptly take steps to identify and resolve problems, without worrying about others' disapproval. They invoke techniques such as majority votes, compromise, and consensus to minimize emotional warfare. Instead of a win/lose approach to problems, they take an integrative approach, in which the resources and positions of all parties are valued. They see conflict as perfectly natural — even as a source of opportunity.

• *Knowing that teamwork isn't all work.* Competent team players recognize that the social element of working life is an important part of the group process. Joking around, "shooting the bull," and otherwise failing to focus 100 percent of one's time and energy on the particular task at hand are frowned upon by some managers, but Grant says these "socio-emotional (or) non-task behaviors" help to relieve tension and boredom. They also help team members understand one another's perspectives. There is a caveat. Successful team players, he says, develop a good sense of timing and appropriateness for the "play" they mix with "work."

• *Having a clear "big picture" perspective.* The most valued members of a team tend to be those who think in terms of how the various participants' roles contribute to the overall group goals. "True team players gain as much satisfaction from group success as they do from individual accomplishments." This frequently means sacrificing one's own interests for the good of the whole team.

• *Attending to group processes.* Finally, effective team players constantly monitor the way the members are working as a team. They are aware that human interaction determines the group's success, and they make it their business to resolve problems and help others improve their team playing skills.

And, one thing that many people don't realize is that *one new person* on a team means that there is now a brand new team. Often a group or team already in existence expects that a new person will just "slide in" and the team will proceed as always. A team leader or team members who don't recognize that there is now a brand new team may be surprised as team dynamics change. Anticipating this change by reorienting the group can avert problems that impede progress and may ultimately affect team spirits.

During a rehearsal at the Metropolitan Opera House in New York City, the great Italian conductor Arturo Toscanini offered a few words of constructive criticism to a featured soloist. The soloist, too proud to accept help, expressed her anger by exploding, "I am the star of this performance!" Toscanini responded calmly but with firm conviction. "Madam," he said, "in this performance there are no stars!"

While relating this story, Jackson Wilson says, "All, from the greatest to the humblest, must work together in harmony and devotion. We can make no advances with only solo work. Unless the soloists and the members of the chorus are ready to work together in harmony, there can be no symphony."

Teamwork has characterized the essence of survival for as long as humans have existed. Yet, it has been more in the areas outside of business. Bolman and Deal explain that "mankind has drawn upon collective resources to do what they could not do alone. United efforts— raising a barn, shoring a levee, rescuing earthquake victims, or singing a hymn — have brought people together, created enduring bonds and exemplified the possibilities of collective spirit."

Effective teams generate positive spirit that will spill over from the collegiality that has developed, the relationships that have formed, and the sense of accomplishment and pride that are the by-products of successful teamwork.

We've discussed the characteristics of a good team member. However, good individual team members don't necessarily make a good team. Assuming that we have those members with the personal characteristics needed, how does team development and team building occur?

Gatto Associates refer to team development and team learning as a "long term approach to helping institute and maintain effective teams that manage themselves and shatter all performance expectations. Team building can help you get new teams off to a great start, get teams that work well together to rise to the level of a high performance team, or help unfreeze and turn around under-performing teams or groups. Team development can help with communication, creativity, problem-solving, teamwork, development of a common goal, team identity, team cohesion, getting to know each other, developing foundations and connections for continuing on the job relationships to enhance your bottom line."

No discussion of team development would be complete without an explanation of the **Stages of Team Development.** This theory predicts that teams, like individuals, pass through predictable, sequential stages over time. The most well known of these models is that of Tuckman (1965) who labeled the stages of team development as forming, storming, norming, performing and adjourning.

Jack Croghan of the University of Miami has broken down Tuckman's theory as follows:

Stage One: Forming

Team begins to form. People find places on the team in relation to one another. "How do I belong?" "How do I get in?" People seek to find out things about one another: attitudes, values, style. Testing continues until one person makes a decision concerning involvement. Team may

Developmental Wheel

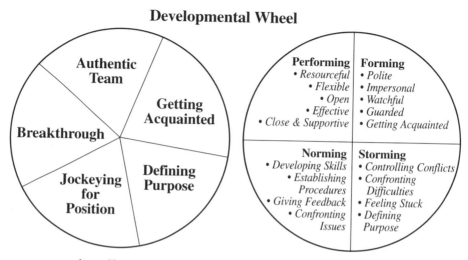

appear to be effective. Initial effectiveness comes from previous attitudes and training. Team should enable each person to get to know other members in a less superficial way.

Stage Two: Storming

Sorting out of personal relationships of power and influence. Alliances are formed, certain people emerge as significant. Team leader has to earn special authority. Team has to decide how it is going to operate. All issues concerned with control. Questions:

- Who controls the team?
- How is control exercised?
- What happens to "delinquents"?

Team needs to work through control issues or they will have difficulty later. Team may appear to make progress, but there is a fundamental weakness.

Stage Three: Norming

Important stage because team needs support and interest of all members. Work of team identified with precision and contributions. Members concerned with *economy of effort* and *task effectiveness*. Ways of talking together developed. Team grows in capacity to handle problems creatively, flexibly, and effectively. Working methods evolve in time. Depth of understanding to be developed.

Stage Four: Performing

Members develop rapport and closeness. Indelible bonds of comradeship forged. Members extend themselves. Informality often typical of team. Roles of team members identified and each person's contribution distinctive. Closeness among team members but open links to others outside team. Difficult to prevent rumors and images from developing.

While Crogan doesn't continue with Stage Five, the original model of Tuckman does address the end of the team.

Stage Five: Adjourning

Teams may adjourn spontaneously or by design. Planned dissolution occurs when the team has completed its task or exhausted its resources. Spontaneous dissolution occurs when members are unable to resolve conflicts, its members grow dissatisfied and depart, or when repeated failure makes the team unable to continue. Either type of dissolution may be stressful. Members of successful teams may not want to end, and when the dissolution is unexpected, members may experience a great deal of conflict or anxiety.

Finally, how do we know if a team is or has been successful? Signs of the team building and team development with effective leadership will be evidenced when the team shows that they:

- Manage conflict
- Have clarified their team purpose
- Develop ideas
- Reach consensus
- Induct new team members effectively
- Make progress toward accomplishing their stated common goal

Harvey Mackay in *Dig Your Well Before You're Thirsty* uses the following story to illustrate the psychological importance and value of teamwork.

> One day a salesman driving on a two-lane country road got stuck in a ditch. He asked a farmer for help. The farmer hitched up Elmo, his blind mule, to the salesman's car. The farmer grabbed a switch, snapped it in the air, and

yelled, "Go Sam, go!" Nothing happened. He snapped it again. "Go Jackson, go!" Still nothing happened. He snapped it again. "Go Jackson, go!" Still nothing. Then he flicked Elmo. "Go Elmo, go!" And Elmo pulled the car out of the ditch.

"Hey, what's with the Sam and Jackson?" asked the driver.

"Look, if he didn't think he had any help he wouldn't even try."

As MacKay concludes, "We all need help. Being part of a team is one way to get it." The business world and leadership training have taken far too long to recognize that individualism, self-reliance and competitiveness are traits that often lead to success, but the spirit generated from a successful team can serve an important function as well. Don't overlook the possibilities that successful teamwork can achieve, and use that spirit for invigoration and unlimited successes!

Bibliography

1. Bolman, Lee G. and Deal, Terrence E., 1995, *Leading with Soul*, Jossey-Bass Publishers, San Francisco, CA.

2. Editorial, *Training*, 1986.

3. Florida Schools Boards Association, Master Board Training, Tallahassee, FL.

4. Gatto Associates, *http://www.teamdevelopers.com*

5. Lowery, Lee and Morgan, Jim, (Texas A & M University), http://asce.tamu.edu/teamings/morgan1/.htm

6. MacKay, Harvey, *Dig Your Well Before You're Thirsty*, 1997, Currency Doubleday, New York, NY.

7. Sergiovanni, Thomas J., *Moral Leadership*, 1992, Jossey-Bass, Inc., San Francisco, CA.

8. Van Ekeren, Glenn, *Words for all Occasions*, 1988, Prentice-Hall, Paramus, NJ.

ABOUT PHYLLIS MAY, PH.D.

*D*r. *Phyllis May has been a teacher, school-based administrator and superintendent of schools. She recently retired after being an educator for 34 years and relocated to Key West, where, as Phyllis describes it, she is beginning Life, Part Deux. With many years of training and practical application in various phases in leadership, she now writes and speaks on effective leadership and education.*

Phyllis stays current on emerging trends as a member of the National Speakers Association, the Florida Speakers Association and various other professional organizations.

Contact Information:
Phyllis May, Ph.D.
P.O. Box 2372
Key West, FL 33045

Phone: (305) 295-7501
Toll free: (877) 312-1800
Fax: (305) 294-7095
E-mail: PmayKeys@mm0.net

TEAMPLAY:
CLUES FOR CREATING COLLABORATIVE TEAMS

by Marianne Frederick, MHSA

W hat does one of the most famous literary mystery duos, Sherlock Holmes and Dr. Watson, have in common with The Motley Fool, one of the most accomplished investment duos? Do unique hats and a creative way of thinking and problem solving immediately come to mind? An affinity for hats is not a prerequisite for successful collaboration, but it may suggest a bolder way of thinking that sets these collaborative teams apart. It's a visual reminder to be willing to look for different ways to stimulate the creative process that fosters insightful, open-minded and successful thinking. I often wear a deerstalker, Sherlock Holmes' favorite hat, and carry a magnifying glass to humorously focus my audiences on the importance of using collaboration to enhance their creative thinking and problem solving abilities.

TeamPlay focuses on appreciating the advantages that diversity provides us in creating collaborative teams. It also embraces the attitude that play is instrumental to the success of both the individual and the group. I often use a fluorescent-orange brain to illustrate that we need more than just our own brainpower to succeed. But in my case, I just don't like to go anywhere without a "spare." If we want to facilitate a learning atmosphere at work and encourage associates to be committed to personal and professional growth, we must teach and inspire collaborative and creative thinking, during which the "spirit of play" is emphasized.

Employees from the three generations of Boomer, Generation 'X' and the Generation 'Y' age associates all verbalize the importance of having workplaces in which they feel that they can enjoy *themselves.*

Generations at Work
Zemke et al., 2000

Today's work force looks at job enjoyment as a necessity, not a perk. If that need is not met, they will move on to other jobs, and losing good workers is something growth-oriented organizations cannot afford. I clearly remember the day I admitted my need to have fun at work after being a workaholic for many years. I was interviewing for a new job and was asked the standard question, "Why are you looking to change jobs?" Well, my gut responded before my brain ever had a chance to shift into gear and I heard myself saying, "Because I'm not having fun anymore where I am now." All I can remember thinking was, "Oh no, I can't believe I said that! What happened to all the well-planned, politically-correct answers I had prepared?" In that instant I realized that I had just told a potential employer of my plans to have fun at work, and he hired me anyway! I have never turned back since uttering that life-changing response nearly seven years ago. I have continued to be true to my life's mission by focusing my energy on teaching people the importance and value of keeping the creative spirit of play in our work life. Participants consistently get that message repeated as I incorporate the word play into most of my program titles and with WorkPlay as my business name.

There are effective ways to build a strong collaborative and creative work team: Processes to encourage members of your team to act, think and coach each other as supportive teammates; procedures to facilitate diversity appreciation and interaction with other members of the team, and actions to help you find a mentor to assist you with your quest for your own successful personal and professional growth. How do you lead your team or a newly forming team to success in each of these endeavors?

You ask them! Barbara Sher describes a **TEAMWORKS!** Team as "a group of people, of any size, called together for the express purpose of helping you get what you want (and getting them what they want in the process)."[1]

What a novel idea, though it's been published in a very old book for a long time, "Ask and you shall receive." The power of collaboration, growth as an organization and personal or professional growth are directly related to your willingness to ask for what you want or need.

It was the day after Thanksgiving, 1977 and a local furniture store was going out of business and auctioning off its entire inventory. I was shopping for a bookcase and dreaming about other pieces that I couldn't afford nor fit into my one-bedroom apartment. There was another buyer, however, and each time I silently picked out a piece of furniture, the auctioneer would bang his gavel, holler "sold" and point to him. He had good taste, I noticed, as he bought an oval-shaped cherry dining room table, chairs and a matching hutch. Later he claimed a queen-sized bed and two matching chests of drawers that appealed to me. I was still clutching my bidding number in my right hand, just itching to flash it at the auctioneer, when the day's bidding came to an end; not a bookcase sold. When I arrived the next morning, and noticed "he" had also returned, I became concerned. Since we obviously liked the same kind of furniture, what if he wanted the bookcase that I had chosen? I decided to scope out the competition and went on a reconnaissance mission to discover his bidding plans. I slowly sauntered over to where he was standing, close enough to speak to him, but without a clue as to how to begin the conversation. Suddenly, in a low, teasing voice, I heard myself saying to him, "I guess I'll just have to move in with you,

[1]*TEAMWORKS!* Sher and Gottlieb (1989)

because you've bought all the furniture that I liked." Needless to say, that got the conversation started! We were married six months later and here it is over twenty years later, and I still have that same furniture and my same favorite husband, Mark. I eventually ended up with not just the one bookcase that I bought (and asked him to help me get to my apartment), but three other bookcases from that auction. See what you can get if you just ask!

Now the rest of you may not be as outspoken or assertive as I am, so asking does not always a relationship create. That takes time, energy and diligence, especially if the other members of the team are very different from you. Learning how to ask the right questions, listening attentively for the answers and discovering how to effectively communicate with people who are not like us, are not often taught in classes. In the work setting more often than not, people are promoted upward because of seniority or through default and are not offered ample opportunities to learn how to carry out their roles as communicators and leaders.

I definitely had no communication training to prepare me for the partnership that began at the furniture auction. People often laugh with me now as I describe some of the hard-earned, gender-related communication lessons that I learned in the early years of being married to someone so different from myself. These stories make humorous learning points as I speak or teach on communication topics, whether it's to women's groups or a gender-mixed audience of team leaders. One day as I was speaking to a group, there was a woman in the back of the room who was obviously enjoying my anecdotes so much that I thought she was going to fall out of her chair laughing. When I approached her after the program, she told me, "The reason it was so funny to me, . . . you kept talking about my husband . . ." Now, I had only told stories about my unique experiences with Mark . . . but she continued, "They act so much alike, they could be brothers!" This gave us both a big laugh, but it also illustrates that there can be some risk in placing people into convenient, stereotypical categories. If we stereotype people, we take a chance on forgetting to focus on their needs as individuals. There is little danger of that happening with Mark, however, because there can't possibly be anyone else in the world with his unique set of idiosyncrasies!

Creating relationships with TeamPlay is the basis for building collaborative partnerships, accomplishing innovative problem solving and expanding our abilities to appreciate and utilize diverse thinking in the workplace.

— TeamPlay
Frederick, 2000

TeamPlay: Beginning of a Model

The *day of the tanks* is my earliest memory of collaborative *teamwork* in action. Living behind and above a toy center has to be every child's dream come true, but in our case it was the family business. From an early age, we learned that the toys (gigantic plush animals) were off limits to us, but that the washer-sized cartons in which they arrived could keep us occupied for hours. How many times have you seen a child be more entertained by the box than by the toy inside of it? That early summer day, a freight truck had arrived with a half-dozen cartons that we had helped Dad empty of their lions, tigers and bears. After wistful looks from huge, brown eyes, Dad finally capitulated to our pleas and deposited three of the more travel-worn boxes out the back door of the warehouse. As the oldest, I naturally led the noisy team deliberations about how to put our new "toys" to best use. Team consensus was eventually reached and a military operation was put into action.

The large size of the boxes enabled two of us kneeling shoulder-to-shoulder on the inside of a box to collaborate in a synchronized crawling motion that successfully maneuvered our "tanks" across the yard, mowing down anything smaller in our path. The youngest neighborhood kids and the dog became the targets of the tank assaults amid much laughter and hollering. I'm also pleased to report that there were no casualties despite three "tanks" crossing paths and colliding in that small backyard. However, the marigolds planted in a border along the edge of the warehouse didn't fare too well that fun-filled afternoon. Later, when engines began running out of gas and knees were nearly rubbed raw from the friction of skin against the inside of the boxes, the three brown tanks lumbered on their final mission across the yard to set up camp outside the kitchen door. There, those grass-stained pieces of cardboard were transformed into picnic areas for the troops and General Mom fed us C-rations in the form of buttered raisin toast. The day of the tanks was full of play, possibilities and teamwork in action. It undoubtedly ignited the spark that became TeamPlay.

Whether it is a team of two or twenty, how can you successfully create partnerships that allow you to achieve your goals? The most important clue is in getting to know people as individuals instead of letting stereotypes get in the way of our relationship building. Often the strengths in our work or personal relationships come from appreciating the diversity of ideas that attitudinal, gender, generational and cultural differences provide to us. Surrounding ourselves with people who are not like us contributes to the growth and vitality of organizations as we strive to become more globally focused in the future.

TeamPlay: A model for achieving successful, collaborative teams at work

• *Create a sense of community:* Community building can be done through the sharing of food, fun and facts. Breaking bread together promotes a sense of camaraderie in a group whether it's in a warehouse, boardroom or a church. Team leaders must model the behavior that they want to see in their staff members, so it's imperative for you to direct the community-building process.

• *Set the right atmosphere:* Set the stage for collaboration and creative thinking by making the environment conducive to your goal, especially if you can't take team members off-site. Props and music will help to set the scene for facilitating any team's creative collaboration. For example, when I do any OSHA and Injury Prevention classes, I wear a white hard hat that reads "OSHA Queen" in metallic-pink lettering. As soon as participants walk through the door, they realize that even mandatory OSHA training can be fun!

• *Encourage fun-filled introductions:* Hats are a great prop both for introductions and to get people talking. You can feel the tension in a room subside, even in a group of strangers, as laughter fills the room. There is usually one flamboyant soul who willingly agrees to choose first from the 100-plus hats that make up my collection. I encourage but don't insist upon their wearing the hats they choose for their introduction.

• *Help people discover each other's strengths:* Diverse thinking is one of the driving forces behind creative collaboration. The "Diversity Game" is a card set that promotes interactivity and serves to facilitate discussions on brain preference, communication and learning or teaching styles. I recommend it to introduce any topic that focuses on why people on a team need to think differently to be successful. It is based on Ned Herrmann's whole-brain theory and contains multiple personality descriptions that relate to brain preference and one's natural strengths. It's an interactive tool for discerning the learning styles of the participants and gives me a quick group assessment so I can adapt my teaching style to fit their needs.

• *Ask people to assess and share their values:* Understanding oneself inevitably leads to understanding others better. Groups often uncover that they have more shared similarities than differences when they discuss values. It begins as a personal exercise and leads to groups discovering values they share or at least a point of reference for improving communication. The focus is to assess how one's values mesh with the organizational mission, and, when or if there isn't a good fit, how changes can be made that lead to increased satisfaction for everyone.

• *Get everyone to contribute to the process:* Group dynamics being what they are, there are those who want to sit back and not be involved and others who dominate the process. Roger vonOech's *Creative Whack Pack* is a valuable tool for facilitating involvement of the participants to stimulate the brainstorming process. A speaker colleague of mine is designing another card set that will help participants focus on their intuitive skills and should prove to be another helpful tool.

   • *Keep their right brains active:* Toys (pardon me, brain-activating tools) help to encourage right brain thinking and keep participants occupied who have trouble sitting still. By keeping hands busy, that nervous energy has an outlet, and the tools contribute to a sense of fun and camaraderie in the group.

   • *Provide brain and body breaks*: An old axiom states "When the body is tired, exercise the mind and when the mind is tired, exercise the body." To this end, games, brainteasers and music are important. My favorites are trivia-type card games, WUZZLES (pictorial brain teasers), word search puzzles (created with inexpensive computer programs) or 30-second mysteries. Physical energies can stagnate with inactivity so music and movement are mandatory. Changing seats reinforces the importance of changing our perspective, and I tell participants it also enables them to enjoy my good looks from a different angle.

Can you turn Team Play into Team Work?

(Change one letter at each step. Can you do it in less than nine steps?)

PLAY _____

　　_____

　　_____

　　_____

　　_____

　　_____

　　_____

　　　　WORK _____

• *Facilitating team fun:* Allowing fun on the team and encouraging group dynamics to evolve without you is a good sign that team synthesis is taking place. Suggest that they create their own energizers, group mixers and brainstorming rules.

• *Fire up their passion:* What can you do to facilitate passion and enthusiasm in the partnership or team? What part of the process excites and motivates each group member? How can we challenge and support one another?

• *Create a vision of the future:* Each team member may have a different mental picture of the goal, mission or vision of the team. Once the team members have the opportunity to share their personal visions, I ask them to create a visual representation of where they are going as a team.

• *Give ideas time to evolve:* Teams may generate sparks of ideas which don't burst into flames until they've been given some time to smolder. Sometimes incubation time is needed, so I encourage people to write down ideas that come to them later in quiet places or after a good night's rest. Where is your best idea-generating location? Mine usually don't surface until I'm in the car or the shower. Initially, the water in the shower kept putting out the flames and washing them down the drain before I could jot them down. One day I found the answer in the form of soap crayons; they work like a charm, but my shower door inevitably ends up looking like a wall of graffiti in New York City.

These are just a few of my favorite tools and techniques for creating collaborative teams; I'm sure you have yours. If I can help you to brainstorm ideas, ignite some sparks to make your collaborative efforts more fun or assist you as you strive to diversify your team thinking, please don't hesitate to contact me. As I sit here typing this chapter into a laptop (I've graduated from yellow legal-pad sheets), it reinforces the issue that our skills in forming collaborative partnerships continue to evolve. We are no longer limited to people with whom we can create face-to-face relationships, but are now expanding our borders and boundaries via the Internet such that we can establish collaborative relationships with anyone around the world. This will require us to develop other innovative ways of building and supporting partnerships and teams into the future. It looks like I'll just have to invest in some virtual hats for **TeamPlay: The Next Generation.**

ABOUT MARIANNE FREDERICK, MHSA

Marianne Frederick laughingly describes her MHSA as her "Masters in Humorously Sharing Anecdotes," although it's her Masters in Health Services Administration from the Medical University of South Carolina. A physical therapist for over twenty years, she has expertise as a health, safety and wellness educator and is an author, professional speaker, humorist and self-proclaimed OSHA Training Queen.

Marianne lives her mission of helping people discover the health, communication and creativity benefits of humor, laughter and play. She leads interactive sessions that encourage learning, refocus thinking and facilitate the growth of intellectual assets of successful organizations, schools, churches and associations. Her clients include: Fluor Daniel, General Nutrition Products, Monsanto and Primedia Workplace Learning.

Contact Information:
Marianne Frederick
WorkPlay, Inc.
14 Bridgewood Ave.
Taylors, SC 29687

Phone: (864) 268-1541
Fax: (864) 268-1541
E-mail: MFredck@aol.com

Treat Customers as People: Think Outside the Self

by Steve Cohn

I grew up in Brooklyn, New York, where a kid spends each day competing, not with hundreds, but with thousands of other kids for space, attention, and a piece of the pie.

There were more than 5,000 kids in my high school. I learned that if I wanted to get ahead or make myself known, I had to have *people on my side*. Having people on my side protected me, kept my life secure, gave me power, helped me grab playground space, insulated me in the constant battle for attention against the new kids on the block, and gave me support when I needed it. It gave me an edge in the competitive atmosphere that comes from living in a metropolitan area of more than 20 million people.

If my childhood situation in Brooklyn sounds like the competitive situation that exists in your market, you're not alone.

Every day we try to maintain or enhance our position in the marketplace. We fight a constant battle for attention against the new kids who are always popping up to compete against us, or against the changes that are an inherent part of doing business. We stress out trying to figure out the best way to reach the most people and sell the most products and services.

What I learned in Brooklyn holds true for all of us. We need to have people on our side. And the best way to get people on your side is to get them to *care* about you. The best way to get them to *care about you* is to show them that you *care about them*. The best way to show them that you *care about them* is to *think outside the self* — to treat people as *people*.

Who are the people we need to have on our side? Our customers. True, real, loyal customers: customers who will stay with you through thick and thin. Customers who will stay with you even if there is a "new kid on the block." Customers who will stay with you even when the other guy drops his prices or changes his product. Customers who will give you the last opportunity to come through when your competitor has made an offer they can't refuse.

How do we get such customers? *By thinking outside the self* — treating people as *people*.

To *think outside the self*, we need to take into consideration other people's wants, needs, desires, and situations and combine them with our own. It's getting away from *what's in it for me* (WII-FM) and instead talking about *what's in it for us?*

Treating people as *people*. Not customers, not employees, not co-workers, not "dollar signs." Treat them as people first, customers later. When we treat people as *people*, people will treat us better, complain less, buy more and come back over and over again.

We Want More Than Satisfied Customers

When *USA Today* recently polled frequent airline passengers on the reasons they choose one airline over another (when they had a choice), the results were quite interesting. More importantly, they were at odds with the way the airline industry usually perceives customers' wants, needs, and situations.

Passengers *did not* choose to fly a particular airline because it had *lower fares*. But every year, we see new, low-priced airlines jump into the fray in an effort to steal away passengers from more established carriers.

Passengers *did not* choose to fly a particular airline because it had better *on-time performance*. But more than one airline has, over the years, positioned itself as the airline with better on-time performance.

Passengers *did not* choose to fly a particular airline because it had *more leg-room* in coach. But one major airline recently began a huge ad campaign touting its increased leg-room.

Passengers chose one airline over another because of *the way they were treated*, often by just one employee.

Good treatment or bad treatment, the actions of one employee can mean the difference between a company with loyal customers and one with customers who come and go. And yet, when the bottom line begins to shake, the first things companies do are to change the product, fix the marketing, or push the salespeople.

What they *should* be doing is starting at the top and teaching each of their people how to treat people as *people* — not customers, not employees, not co-workers, not "dollar signs." Treat people as *people* first, customers later.

A well-known customer service statistic says that 68 percent of all customers who switch to another business do so because of the way *they were treated.* Only 14 percent move because they were unhappy with the product.

There are companies that brag about how many *satisfied* customers they have. Satisfied customers will jump as soon as they're given reason to. Is it a new and lower price? New location? Internet? New format? In order to change satisfied customers into loyal customers, we need to do more.

We need to enhance their experiences. When customers purchase our products or services, they are paying for experiences, not products. Their experiences are not only based on how the product succeeds at what it was supposed to do, but more often on the way the company takes care of them. Especially when something goes wrong.

Here are 10 ways to enhance those experiences by treating customers as *people*.

1. Treat customers like family.

A participant in one of my *Delighting Customers* classes told me of a neighbor of his who worked in a Ford auto dealership for 45 years. People came to him for their cars over and over again, and brought their kids in when it was time for their first cars.

Time moves on, and eventually "Tom" retired. People came to the dealership and asked "Where's Tom?" When told he had retired, they talked of how Tom had treated them like family — taking interest in their stories, their ups, their downs, and their lives. They told how they always got a Christmas card and cards for their family members' birthdays.

Many told of naming Tom as a godparent for their kids. Tom's wall was always filled with pictures of his "children" and "grandchildren."

The people asked for Tom so often that the dealership asked if he would come back. Tom was enjoying his retirement, but consented to come in three days a week, just to greet and be like family to the dealership's customers. Though Tom never made another sale, the dealership's sales went up dramatically.

We need to treat the customer as family — people who will stay on our side no matter what changes come. We need to treat customers as people we want to see and/or speak with over and over again — people we wouldn't think of treating badly or with indifference.

We want to treat them as *people*. When we treat them as *customers* we separate them from the rest of humanity. Treat them well, not because they're customers, but because they're people who deserve to be treated well. Treat them that way because it's the right thing to do.

2. Treat every person as if he or she is the only person in the world.

My old friend, Norman Liss, was a long-time public relations consultant who worked for companies of all sizes. When I began my business, he gave me some sage advice: "If there's anything I've learned during the 40 years I've been in business, it's this: Never let your client know you have any other clients. Don't ever tell them that something couldn't be done because you were busy with someone else. When you are dealing with them, be thinking about them. When you're talking with them, don't make them feel you'd rather be somewhere else, or with someone else. Treat the $10 client like a million-dollar client. Treat the million-dollar client like your best friend."

Customers want to be treated as if they're special. Most of the time, they don't even know they want to be treated that way. It is your job to treat them that way, anyway. After you do what you say you're going to do, always ask yourself, "What else can I do?"

Let them know you are with them from start to . . . whenever. Constantly reassure them that you are going to help them and that you are happy to help them.

3. Trust people to handle the truth.

Over the years, I have found that most people and companies don't trust people to handle the truth.

I was traveling from Newark Airport to Atlanta on a Friday night not long ago. The airline I was traveling with has these small bag-meals, which usually contain a sandwich, a cookie (love those cookies!), a small bottle of water and a bag of chips. The airline gives these to dinner-time coach passengers on the way into the plane, on flights of anywhere from an hour-and-a-half to two hours-and-a-half. We don't get a full meal. I understand.

On this particular Friday, I had been training all day. I was tired and hungry. My flight was to take off at 7:25 p.m. I arrived at the airport at approximately 6:35 p.m. after fighting off New Jersey Turnpike traffic.

I had a little less than an hour before my flight. I looked at my ticket and saw a fork and knife symbol, indicating that food was to be served, in some fashion.

When my row was called, I proceeded to the gate, grabbed my meal bag and found my seat. About a half-hour later, I reached into my bag to find two breadsticks, a small, round container of cream cheese, and the aforementioned cookie and water. Though I ate it, my stomach rumbled the rest of the way home.

Months later, when doing some consulting for this same airline, I mentioned this story. I asked why I wasn't told in advance what was in the bag. One of the people I was talking to said, "Between you and me, we don't want to get the passengers thinking about the food. They're upset enough that they're no longer getting a full meal. So, we say as little about the food as possible."

Interestingly, I would have been less upset if I had known what was in the bag. If I had known that all I was getting was breadsticks and cream cheese, I might have bought a sandwich at the airport and taken it on the plane. I can handle the truth.

Give me control over my own situation. Let me make my own decisions about what I need to do. Let me know what's happening. Treat me like a person.

People like to know what is happening and what is happening next. As humans, we have this incredible desire to see the future. It makes us feel secure. We like to know where we're going. Even if the news is bad, we want to know.

We also want to know why.

4. Explain why. Explain simply.

My daughter's school bus schedule was changed. I called the bus dispatch supervisor to find out why. He refused to tell me.

We talked for 45 minutes. I kept asking him why the schedule needed to be changed. He kept giving me every reason why I didn't need to know. I got the feeling he decided to make the change just to annoy me. I couldn't come up with any other reason why the schedule had been changed.

He told me there were many reasons and that he couldn't go into them. Then he told me that I didn't need to know why. The change had to be done.

I persisted. Finally, he said, "Mr. Cohn, why do you need to know why?" I said, "Because if you tell me why, I might understand and go with you on this. If it's a good reason and it makes sense, I have no argument and I'll politely get off the phone. If I find a hole in your reasoning, I might be able to give you some information to change your mind."

The reason he finally gave me (after 40 minutes!) was rational and made sense. I was also able to give him some information that would allow him to go back to the original schedule the next year. He appreciated that.

(What I didn't tell him was that my wife had asked me to make the call. I also needed to be able to tell *her* the reason for the change, and I wasn't getting off the phone until I knew!)

Why did he refuse to give me a reason? Because he was afraid that I wouldn't understand or accept his reason. Perhaps he was right. But that is no excuse not to tell me.

He did not treat me like a person. He treated me like a pain-in-the-butt who did not have the capacity to understand. He didn't trust that I would accept the truth.

When you tell people why, they are more likely to support you in what you are doing. The people you call your customers are responsible for your success. They decide whether you succeed or fail. If you don't trust them with the truth, they think you're hiding something. Nobody wants to support somebody who hides.

Also, explain simply. Use words the person understands. Keep away from jargon. Make it simple. People who hear you use big words and long explanations don't think you're smart. They think you're not listening.

5. Feel their pain.

During the recession of 1992, a New Hampshire woman told then-candidate Bill Clinton a tale of woe brought on by the poor economy. With wet eyes, the future President embraced the woman and said his now famous words "I feel your pain."

The words appeared in political humor throughout Clinton's administration, but the truth is that he touched on something deep in each of our hearts. When we have pain, we want others to feel it.

We need to accept people's pain. Show them you feel their pain by empathizing with their situation. State that you are there to help. If you have seen the situation before, tell them so and tell them what can be done. If you have *been* in the situation before, tell them. They will understand that you understand.

Most importantly, empathize *before* you begin to solve their problem. Show them you care about them first. Then solve the problem.

6. Show them that you care about them. Ask lots and lots of questions.

Everybody wants others to pay attention to them. The more attention we pay to a person, the more that person will want to be with us. Remember what we said earlier: The best way to get people to be on your side is to show them that you care about them. We can show we care about them by asking questions.

When you ask questions, you are showing interest in their situation. Whatever your stake in the matter, you give it up when you ask others questions. They understand that you are interested in their point of view or their opinion. They understand that you are listening. And everybody loves people who listen.

Listening is the most powerful tool you can use in any person-to-person situation, customer-oriented or not. People flock to people who listen.

Ask as many questions as you need to until you get the information you need. Make sure you have all the information you need to help the person. If there is anything you are assuming, make sure you ask a question to clarify it. Don't take information for granted. It may not be so.

But don't interrogate. Preface your questions with information that tells people you're going to ask a question. Say, "Let me ask you some questions," or "Can I ask you about . . .?"

Conversationally, questions can be perceived as an attack. You are making other people do something they weren't prepared to do. You asked a question and now they have to answer. They may not want to answer. So let them know you're going to ask a question before you ask. It gives them control. People like control.

7. Don't treat people as dollar signs.

There was an old Bugs Bunny cartoon in which Bugs looks at Elmer Fudd and Elmer turns into a giant lollipop. On the round, candy part of the lollipop is written *SUCKER*.

Sometimes I think that most of us treat our customers on the basis of how much money they are bringing to us. As Bugs Bunny saw Elmer Fudd as a giant sucker, we see our customers as giant "dollar signs." We see customers as having no lives, no personalities, no needs, and no reason to exist other than their ability to make us money. Customers can pick up this attitude and they resent it.

Customers are not "dollar signs." They are people with wants, needs, desires, and situations. We need to treat them as the *people* they are. As my friend Norman said, "Treat the $10 client like a million-dollar client. Treat the million-dollar client like your best friend."

8. Never tell anyone what you can't do.

Even if you can't do what the customer wants you to do, tell them what you *can do*. There's always something you can do.

The most devastating words in customer caring are "I can't do that," or "That's not possible." Would you say those words to people you really cared about? Or would you try to find a way to make them happy? My bet is that you would choose the latter.

There's always something we can do, including finding another provider to sell them the same type of product.

If you acknowledge the customer's needs and let them know that you would like to help, you can then offer an alternative to what they asked for. The customer is not always right or entitled. But the customer is always important. The customer is always a person first.

9. Go out of your way for people. Do the things others won't do.

I walked into my local hardware store. I am the first to admit that I don't know the first thing about "doing-it-yourself." I needed to fix my shower faucet.

The fellow behind the counter explained to me how to fix the faucet and sold me the materials I needed. I went home and tried. It wasn't working.

It turned out I needed a particular kind of wrench to fix the faucet. The wrench was not cheap. The fellow behind the counter offered to let me borrow his wrench if I would bring it back later that day.

I brought it home, fixed the shower and returned it. I never needed the same wrench again. I also continued to shop in that store, even when the super-hardware store opened up nearby.

Was he the cheapest guy in town? No. Did he have the biggest selection? No. Was he the closest in proximity to my house? No.

I remained his customer because he showed faith in me as a person. He showed faith that I would bring back his expensive tool. He treated me as a person. He didn't worry that I wasn't a "do-it-your-selfer." He didn't see the dollar signs. He went out of his way for me. So I went out of my way for him.

It costs five times more to find a new customer than to keep an old one. Can we really afford to let even one customer go away?

10. Never take it personally. This is not about you.

I had a woman in one of my classes who told me that she hangs up on the customer anytime the customer starts to scream, yell, or curse.

"I tell him, 'Sir, I will not listen to this. If you insist on cursing at me, I will hang up!'" she said. The caller, of course, continued to curse. And she hung up.

I asked her, "Do you think your statement made the caller *calmer* or *angrier*?" She replied that it didn't matter; she was not going to be talked to that way.

It does matter. A cursing caller is angry — not at you, but at something. He or she may be angry with any number of things, including the situation, your company, the fact that the situation has happened before, or he or she may be angry with the last person he or she spoke to at your company. It may be any number of things, the least of which is you.

The caller's cursing is not about you. It's about the situation and it's about what happened to the caller. All the caller wants is attention. You can give that caller attention by asking questions.

Questions diffuse anger. But remember, bridge to your questions. When the caller curses, say, "Sir, I would like to help you with your situation. Do you mind if I ask you a few questions so I can better understand what happened?" The caller will probably continue to curse at this point. Follow his or her cursing with, "I understand you're very upset. If I can ask you a couple of questions, I'm sure I'll be able to help." Then ask the caller as many questions as you can until he or she calms down. In addition, constantly state your desire to help.

Confrontation doesn't help anybody. Caring about customers is not about you. It's about the *person* who needs help, needs you to understand, and/or needs you to feel his or her pain.

Far too often, we see the world as *us* and *them*. We see other people as being there for us. We listen to the radio station WII-FM — what's in it for me?

While it may be a fact of life that people think of themselves first, and then think of others, it is no way to get people on your side. Treat people as *people* by *thinking outside the self* — taking into consideration their wants, needs, desires, and situations and then combining them with your own — and you will have people who are loyal to you and your company forever.

ABOUT STEVE COHN

teve Cohn is a speaker, seminar leader, writer and consultant who teaches people how to communicate with, sell to and best serve customers through increased caring, insight and thinking outside the self. He demonstrates that the best way to increase the bottom line is by connecting with others as people, not merely customers, clients, employees or dollar signs.

Steve shares his unique perspectives on human nature, gained as an award-wining radio and print journalist with United Press International, the Associated Press and NBC. His popular keynote, Treat People as People, inspires and motivates participants to care about each other as the foundation for building more successful businesses, better relationships and happier lives. His clients include Delta Airlines, AT&T, BellSouth, Carolina Power & Light, and the U.S. Department of Housing and Urban Development. Steve serves on the Board of Directors of the Georgia Speakers Association and is a member of the National Speakers Association.

Contact Information:
Steve Cohn
Absolutely Delightful Dreamers
560 Summer Breeze Court
Alpharetta, GA 30005

Phone: (770) 667-3042
Fax: (770) 667-3142
E-mail: ADDreamers@aol.com

MASTER MINDS AND THE MIND MAINTENANCE PROGRAM: THE SECRET TOOLS FOR MASTERING CHANGE

by Lisa Bell

"The Master Mind Principle holds the secret of the power wielded by men who surround themselves with other men of brains."
—Napoleon Hill,
Think and Grow Rich

Master Minds and the Mind Maintenance Program provide the knowledge and the tools to create the wealth you want and deserve in both your personal and professional lives. The Master Mind process clarifies your focus, moves your life forward and helps you get what you want. New business leaders would benefit greatly from the concept though few make use of this precious idea. Just as you provide proper maintenance for your car, the Mind Maintenance Program provides that extra boost to help your mind work more efficiently.

There is give and take in any project. So it goes with the Master Mind process. The rewards, however, far exceed the costs, as you will see. The "teamwork" bond is one of the many perks received from participating in a Master Mind. My Master Mind members are life-long friends whom I can contact anytime. The trust and integrity born out of our group has created a sincere bond of closeness. Time passed between conversations is irrelevant. While Master Mind is a group concept, the

Mind Maintenance Program encompasses your personal arena. Both are invaluable. I know. They saved my business.

In the fall of 1995 I chose to become one of those "entrepreneurs" and, in search of that American Dream, opened my own business. I had in the early 80's operated a successful balloon delivery service complete with tuxedo-grams, circus clowns and the most popular, "bellygrams." It was a glorious time when family members pitched in and business was booming. With mom as my secretary and our seventy-year-old, next door neighbor Julia as my traveling bodyguard, I was, in retrospect, a true entrepreneur. I was a teacher during the day and a businesswoman after school hours. Changing times and the choice of relocating to a warmer climate ended the extensive era of "Lisa's Belle-A-Gram Service." It was time to move on.

Fifteen years later I was ready to try again. As a teacher I had been out of the business world. The rules had changed. With my financial support I chose to have my business partner handle all the business transactions. What kind of business you ask? After a while, I, myself, wondered. Initially a conference and seminar production company, we did what we thought was our "marketing research." We bought *one* book. We knew that book inside out. On the roller-coaster ride of expenses versus revenue, again, my partner handled all the business transactions. After all, I was a teacher. What did I know about the changing business world? Do you see a picture forming? In retrospect, our inexperience showed. It was also about to cost us a lot of money. I remember quite clearly my partner's words, "Lisa, to make money, you have to spend money." I agreed. I just did not think it was going to be *that* much money, *my money*. Two years later and financially devastated, I took a long hard look at what had happened. Accepting where the company had been, I set out to reinvent my business, minus a business partner. Global Connections Speakers Bureau has been evolving ever since. Quitting was not an option. Focus was everything. In reflecting, my Master Mind plus a strategy called the Mind Maintenance Program were both the pivotal points in my business. I had made some serious mistakes. I am here to prevent you from making those same mistakes. Listen and listen well.

You've chosen to be your own boss. WOW! Great idea. I have some good news and some bad news for you. First the bad news. This is Statistics 101. Over seventy percent of new business ventures fail in their first two years. Most new businesses, small businesses, are not prepared for what is ahead of them. The good news: This survival rate has been improving over recent years. Why? The "Information Revolution" has allowed us to work harder at preparing and increasing the chances of succeeding. To ensure entrepreneurial growth and success we must face the fact that we cannot do it all alone. Seeking perspectives from different angles helps to create that winning perception of looking at the "whole picture." In his book, *Think and Grow Rich*, Napoleon Hill reinforced the term "Master Mind," first coined by Andrew Carnegie. Expanding to the next level, the Mind Maintenance Program creates the "inner dialogue" necessary to focus in the direction you want to go. It provides the *plan*.

What are Master Minds? Take your seven to ten most respected business/personal colleagues, provide an encouraging environment, add a little challenge and lots of trust, and watch the magic begin. Having "like minded " people in one room together generates a new force where all who give, receive. I am not talking about surrounding yourself with "yes" men either. Quite the opposite. Devil's advocates, different perspectives, and general business knowledge initiate the creative dialogue to develop new ideas.

A strong source of energy, the Master Mind creates a concentrated harmony designed to assist all that actively participate. There is something in it for everyone, too. All bring to the table their advice, counsel and personal cooperation. All leave with so much more. According to Napoleon Hill's book, *Think and Grow Rich*, Andrew Carnegie's Master Mind consisted of a staff of about fifty men with one common purpose

— the manufacturing and marketing of steel. The fact is that coming together and functioning harmoniously toward a common good creates an alliance that generates the energy to move that mind to the next level. The next level is the Mind Maintenance Program. It is the *how* to move to the next level.

The recipe for a successful Master Mind is simple: time, people and desire. However, the one ingredient that can make or break the whole process involves *commitment*. This includes the commitment from the members to give of their expertise and receive feedback graciously, the commitment to be "in the moment" while at the meeting and to accept all comments amiably, and the commitment to respect the ground rules established by all who participate. The ground rules established for the Master Mind will vary while the general objectives are always the same: to generate ideas and possible solutions for the members' concerns at hand. After a while, just as with brushing your teeth and eating breakfast, the Master Mind meeting becomes a necessary part of your schedule.

Having worked with Master Minds in the past, I have learned that many formats are available. Meeting weekly, every two weeks, or once a month for a given amount of time can work. Each person brings to the table one specific issue for that meeting that we tackle from different perspectives. The end result you can accept or not. You will, however, leave with a broader spectrum of knowledge on your issue. The Master Mind works as one unit for each issue/problem presented. Within the time restraints you will find the time for all to benefit from the process.

Location for Master Mind sessions can vary. Is it important? You bet. At my favorite Master Mind meeting, I was sitting next to a beautiful lake sipping a glass of champagne. Get the picture? This is *not* work, this is *fun*. So often we forget as adults how to play and enjoy ourselves. Ease off the pressure and watch the creativity flow.

The Mind Maintenance Program involves a process called the Seven C's Strategy. Once implemented, this process clarifies your plans and provides the focus needed to remain on your journey. Add the Master Mind dimension to this equation and amazing things begin to happen. In the Mind Maintenance Seven C's Strategy Program, our first "C" is one of identification. The ability to clearly see the challenge that lays ahead of you can be overwhelming. With so much extraneous "stuff" going on around you, deciphering what is important is not as easy as you think. Clarification of your challenge sets you in the right direction. The process requires active participation, so take out your pens and paper. No one said this would be a free ride.

Challenge: What's the issue? Financial, personal, business related? Write it down. Seeing it on paper makes it real. Visual reinforcement is a powerful one. Work on only one challenge at a time. The ripple effect could provide insight into other issues. Identifying the specifics can be downright painful but it is essential to begin the process.

Our second "C" is one of reflection. After identifying the challenge, in your next step look for options, your choices. During Master Mind discussions, new choices will arise. All should be addressed with no stone left unturned.

Choices: You'll need more paper here. Write down all the choices you have regarding your challenge. Yes, write down *all* of them. Write down even the most extreme of choices. While you might initially be "stuck" for ideas, once you begin to write, other choices will begin to flow. Within each choice label one side "+" for the positives and the other side "-" for the negatives relating to the choice. This means writing down the good and the bad associated with your choice. Keep listing until you have exhausted all your reserves. Your Master Mind will keep you writing. They will provide both the positives and the negatives from their perspectives. If it doesn't happen immediately, put the project aside and come back to it later. Soon you will see patterns emerging. Patterns of choices you might want to explore in more detail. You will also eliminate other possibilities. The Mind Maintenance Program doesn't happen all at once. Again, Mind Maintenance continues where the Master Mind ends.

The third "C" is one of obligation. Here is where many falter and fail to complete the process. A tough word for some, while for others, the true meaning is never really understood.

Commitment : You have done your homework. The lists have been prepared and meticulously reviewed. Your Master Mind has provided you with multiple viewpoints on the subject. Now, you must *act*. The commitment to your choice is the pivotal point of the Mind Maintenance Program. Here is where many may fall short of their goals. For some reason, either internally or externally, many have trouble following through. They just quit too early. The question here is, "What are you willing to do to make things work?" Careful. It is a loaded question filled with many levels of commitment. These levels will surprise you. The Master Mind support helps here. Obligation to your Master Mind is great for keeping you on track. This is also the point where many people drop out of the Master Mind.

This "C" is one of planning. The time frame, action plan and perceived outcomes are all yours. Master Mind may assist, but only *you* know what is best for you. The Mind Maintenance Program requires that you develop an internal dialogue through which you systematically approach and expand your knowledge.

Charting : How will you get there? Charting a course before you leave the harbor is the sign of an experienced captain. While the Master Mind provides the ideas of how to solve your problems at hand, generating the specific "how to project" is a personal plan. Individualized "action plans" are tailored to meet your specific needs. Small incremental steps/goals provide the "inch by inch, it's a cinch" approach. Sharing with the Master Mind is a great idea, but ultimately you must implement the steps. The process of organizing the steps to achieve success is your major project. Rewards of various types provide the encouragement to continue in your direction.

Using a piece of paper held horizontally, draw one big line across the paper. At the far left of your paper label "present." At the far right label "future." At your present end of the paper write your current age. At the future side of the paper put the number 77. This is your estimated time line remaining here on earth. Dividing into five year increments, the sobering effect of numbers hits home. Where do you want to be in five years? At first glance the increments look a bit short. *And you are dead right.* With the average life span of an American approximately 77 years old, God willing, charting these waters takes time and effort. Mind you, it is all speculation too. Calculated speculations that will direct you toward your goals. Take your challenge and list it at the present end. Note the distance from the present/challenge end to the opposite of 77 years. Sometimes the distance will look miles away while other times it will seem only inches. Carrying your challenge the whole length of the time line is burdensome. Give it a deadline. Otherwise it will rule your life. The truth of the matter is you can carry that challenge the whole length of your time line or you can work at diversifying your life event portfolio. To carry or not to carry — that is the question. Once you answer that question, you start looking at options and start charting the course of action. This strategy includes using small, measurable and immediate goals working towards the long-term, successful end result. List the small, immediate and attainable goals that will bring you to your desired point. Beware of the realities of life interfering with your greatest of plans. Ability to adjust your sails is a must.

The next "C" has been so underestimated. Conveying what you want to those around you involves high quality speaking skills, and more importantly, great listening skills. It is the listening to the what not the whom, that counts.

Communicating: Conveying your message to those around you sounds quite easy. You figure, you just *tell* them. Wrong, dead wrong. While the skill of choosing words and fluently declaring your intentions is important, the art of listening not only to whom, but to what is happening around you requires skill of the highest degree. I have always found that I have learned much more when I am *listening* rather than speaking. The art of "active listening" provides a foundation for using the cues and the knowledge that surrounds us for our own personal and professional growth. We never stop learning the art of improving our communication skills. A powerful asset, the Master Mind process requires that we remain active in the listening process while the Mind Maintenance program *demands* it.

In the Mind Maintenance program, the next "C" is one of ingenuity.

Creativity: No one ever found new ideas looking in the same old places. Let me clarify that. No one ever found new ideas looking at the same old problems with the same old *mindset*. Delving deep into the imagination generates energy that "snowballs." Unleashing the creative process releases the child within. The child within thinks quite differently. Free of restraints, boundaries and certainly self-evaluations, the child within somehow was lost as we matured. The child within is still there. In the creative process of reawakening this child, our own "personal tape recordings" reappear. These are the tapes reminding us of our perceived limitations and personal shortcomings. These personal tapes are tough to reprogram . . . but doable. It takes the investment of work and time. You are worth it. Besides, what is the alternative? Listening to these past, pre-programmed tapes that prevent you from achieving what you want serves no purpose. Replacing these tapes with new affirmations of achievement will serve to reinvent yourself and your future. No boundaries, no restraints and certainly no self evaluations, releasing the child within recreates your inner core while initiating a self-mastery program that will provide unlimited growth. The Mind Maintenance Program assists you in reawakening this inner child while the Master Mind harnesses the power you rediscover.

The final "C" of Mind Maintenance is one of transformation. An ongoing progression, the Mind Maintenance Program draws from all the other Seven C's to help us conquer the fear of the inevitable: *change*. While it throws many off track, creates anxiety and makes many uncomfortable, change is, truly, what makes the world go round.

Change: This is the ultimate reason for participating in the Master Mind. Having completed the Mind Maintenance Program, you are now at your next level and probably welcome change. Creating the desired change is the next focus. Along the journey the desired change might have begun to take on a new look. What about when life steps in? Call it fate, life, whatever; sometimes life just throws that glitch in your plans mentioned earlier. It happens to the best of us. Life readjusts our sails in another direction. You will find that your *flexibility*, the ability to adjust, will be the powerful key to the level of success. Time, flexibility and self-evaluation will keep you on your toes.

There are *universal principles of change* that cannot be denied. These universal principles of change, when recognized, allow us to be the person in the moment while developing the person we will become. From the rearranging of priorities to finding the "golden nuggets" along the way, the process of change compels us to rediscover both the good and bad in ourselves. It also allows us the leeway in accepting our less than glorious attributes and allows us to work on proposing new directions for the future.

The Mind Maintenance Program and Master Mind also encourage the development of strong leadership skills. Kahlil Gibran once said, "The truly great man is he who would master no one, and who would be mastered by none." Quiet influence, personal guidance, integrity, vision are all addressed in the Mind Maintenance Program. Leaders seek other leaders. They surround themselves with those that will provide nourishment for mind, body and soul. They avoid toxic people. And there are many of them out there.

What does all this mean? This process produces results — results that will affect your circle of influence while creating new dimensions in you as a person. You are reinventing yourself. With the focus of the Mind Maintenance Program and the assistance from the Master Mind, watch what happens. Every day I am reminded of where I want to go with my business. The direction, grounding and sense of continuity both programs provide helps me continue on my mission. I place reminders of my personal and professional goals all around the office . . . on the lateral filing cabinet, on the computer and yes, even on the bathroom door. I use little blue circular "stickies." Reminders are cues to keep me on track in a fast-paced world where I can so easily be distracted. To the ordinary eye they are just blue dots; to me they are reminders of where I want to go with Global Connections Speakers Bureau and, better still, where I want to go with Lisa Bell.

ABOUT LISA BELL

*L*isa Bell helps individuals in corporations, associations and educational organizations develop the necessary leadership skills to implement the changes they face. A successful business owner and community leader, Lisa is President of the Southern Chapter for ALS/Lou Gehrig's disease and serves on the boards of directors for the South Florida chapter of Meeting Professionals International and the Florida Speakers Association.

　　Through her radio show, Live Like You Really Mean It!, Lisa brings hope and help to thousands of listeners and dishes up humor to help people deal with life's adversities. Her company, Global Connections Speakers Bureau, works closely with corporations and associations help match them with speakers who are the best for making their important meetings smashing successes.

Contact Information:
Lisa Bell
Global Connections Speakers Bureau
4631 NW 31st Ave., Suite 166
Fort Lauderdale, FL 33309

Phone: (954) 972-5515
Fax: (954) 972-0641
E-mail: GlobalWiz@aol.com
Web: www.GlobalConnections.com

Balancing Your Act: Sandy's Pointers for Reducing Stress

by Sandy Pointer, M.S.W., LCSW

The line at the supermarket wasn't moving but I could not help but smile as I noticed the lady at the head of it. On the back of her tee shirt was the boldly emblazoned message, "I'M TOO BLESSED TO BE STRESSED." What a powerful attitude for handling life's daily challenges. I was impressed! That is until I realized the line was stalled because this blessed being was bawling out the baffled cashier. She didn't take it well that an item she wanted was out of stock. After all, she had a coupon! As she stomped out of the store in distress, I thought, this woman (I no longer refer to her as a lady) needed to turn her tee shirt around so that with a glance down she could be reminded of her state of blessedness. She obviously needed to be reminded. There was no doubt that her manner was incongruent with her message. Do you have a message? If so, what is it? Moreover, does your manner match your message?

Stress

Stress affects behavior and communication and can be positive or negative. Positive stress can be a catalyst that relentlessly drives us around, over or through obstacles to the successful completion of a goal or task. Negative stress can fuel negative outbursts as observed in the woman in the supermarket. Our stress level is largely measured or determined by the extent to which we create stressful situations — overextending ourselves, making poor decisions, having unrealistic expectations of ourselves or others, and the manner in which we choose to react to what we interpret as stressful situations.

Like a car whose wheels are knocked out of alignment following an accident, too much stress can knock us out of balance as well. Just as a car must be balanced to operate effectively, we must manage stress in order to find and maintain balance in our lives and reach our optimal level of performance. Your car does not have to be involved in an accident, nor do you have to experience a major life crisis to arrive at a state of imbalance. Everyday wear and tear from those numerous little bumps in the road is sufficient to require conscientious vehicle realignment. We need to frequently realign or readjust our priorities and schedules in order to achieve success and balance between countless professional demands and personal responsibilities — our homes, family members, fulfilling our spiritual needs and obligations, engaging in healthy social relationships, and taking care of our physical and emotional needs. Wow! Do you sometimes feel like you are juggling more balls than you can manage? When you "drop the ball" — just one, do you experience guilt and even more stress? Then read on.

This chapter supports the value of positive relationships or teams in enhancing your success. It provides several "Pointers" to help you to be a more effective team player, reduce stress, and achieve a more balanced and enjoyable life. My "Pointers" are based on common life experiences and the lessons I've learned from them.

Team Communication

A team is simply two or more positive, supportive, cooperative relationships who have a common goal(s). It can be a husband and wife, family members, friends, small or large groups and professional work teams. Sometimes, though, the communication between team members gets blurry. If unclear, communication can be a source of stress. Misunderstandings that result from poor communication can fracture relationships, inhibit achievement, and can even be fatal. However, when language is used effectively, besides reducing stress, it can strengthen relationships and help us successfully complete our goals. Good, clear and timely communication is a vital factor in reducing stress.

Sandy's Pointers

My first Pointer follows this cute story I love about the importance of good clear communication. A man who was a great pet lover worked across the street from a pet store. Frequently, he would browse in the store during his lunch hour. The pet owner knew that he particularly loved birds. One day he entered the pet store and the owner greeted him excitedly. He informed him that a very rare talking bird had been delivered just that morning. "This bird can speak five languages," said the owner, "five different languages." The man doubted this was possible; but sure enough he listened as the bird chattered in fluent English, French, German, Japanese, and Spanish. Fascinated beyond words, the man knew he had to have the bird. He wrote the $500 check required and handed it to the owner. "I have a meeting right after work," he said "so please deliver the bird to my home address on the check." The man couldn't wait to get home. As he opened the door to his house, he was greeted with a "fowl" aroma. "What smells so good?" he asked his wife. "Oh, I roasted that bird you had delivered this afternoon," she responded. The man was shocked and appalled. "That was a rare, intelligent, and expensive bird," he scolded. "That bird could speak five languages, do you understand? — five different languages." The wife, unimpressed, looked at her husband and replied, "If he was so smart, and could do all that speaking, when I was putting him in the oven, why didn't he speak up?"

Pointer #1 Know when to speak up and when to shut up!

Determine when the communication of your impressions, concerns, and convictions is appropriate and when it is preferable to refrain from comment.

This "multi-lingual bird," while able to speak many languages, did not understand any of them. He was only able to repeat what he had heard; therefore, he did not know when to squawk or when to hush. He was unable to use language to empower himself which brought fatal results. The poor bird went from being stressed out to being stretched out, literally.

An Ashanti proverb says, "True power comes through cooperation and silence." How do you know when to speak up and when to shut up? You know when you increase your level of awareness. Learn to be extra attuned to what is going on around you. Take a penetrating look! Managers and other people who are successful at forming and maintaining positive relationships or teams know how to read other people and situations. Watch for signs: verbal cues, facial expressions, body language, and behavioral indicators. When possible, address the root issues in situations before they become overheated. Timing is of great importance.

Timing also plays a significant role when it comes to silence. In some situations, such as following loss, silent support — just being there, is often all that is needed. In other situations, it is better to remain silent until you have obtained sufficient information to make a decision or confront another. Silence is always preferable to an angry response. However, silence can be insulting when a response is expected or required. If you are angry, rather than to ignore a person, it is better to set a time to meet later, allowing you the opportunity to calm down.

In some situations, silence implies consent. Silence can also imply disinterest. A couple years after I became a widow, I was faced with a rather big financial decision. My late husband, Emritt, had been the better manager and I wasn't sure what to do or where to seek sound advice. While discussing this one evening, I said to my younger daughter, "I wish Daddy would send me a sign, send me an answer." She quickly, but lovingly replied, "He didn't answer you when he was alive." We both chuckled. One of the things I "challenged" Emritt about in the earlier years of our marriage was his frequent failure to answer, or even acknowledge that he had heard my question. Eventually, I realized that he wasn't ignoring me, he wasn't disinterested, he was "processing." When he finished, I would get an answer. Sometimes, by the time I got the answer, I would have forgotten the question. But his answer, when it came, would always reflect serious thought. Sometimes it would include results from his research on the issue, and most always it would be just what I wanted or needed to hear. He was the same with our daughters. Certain of his love and dedication, we learned to just accept his "unique" style of communication. It also decreased stress for all of us.

To reduce stress, when the decision is made to speak up, be sure to:

Know what to say. Choose what to say and know what it means. Don't be like the bird and just repeat what you have heard. Increase your knowledge as well as your vocabulary and be willing to share that knowledge with others in a caring way.

Know whom to say it to. Approach the correct person, talk to, instead of about the person and never forget to give praise to whom it is due. The woman in the supermarket should have directed her complaints to the manager, not the cashier who simply rings up the items. She wouldn't have held up the line that way either.

Know how to say it. The value of tact cannot be overstated. However, everyone has those times when they say the wrong thing. One question I've learned not to ask is "When is your baby due?" Three times I've received the answer, "I'm not expecting!" What to say after that can be challenging. But, in these situations, I've discovered that it's not what I say, but the sincerity in which I say it. When people realize that you care and that you are more hurt and embarrassed than the hurt and embarrassment you caused them, they are usually forgiving.

My second Pointer to help you reduce stress and achieve balance, follows this story. When I was a little girl, I would watch my dear grandmother perform various tasks in the kitchen. Making fresh orange juice was one of those tasks. First, she'd place about a half dozen oranges on the kitchen table. Next, she'd methodically knead each one before cutting them in halves. Then, she'd press, roll and squeeze each orange half on the top of the glass juicer over and over again until all of the juice was extracted. The juice, pulp, and seeds dribbled into the shallow bowl of the juicer. When the bowl of the juicer filled, she gently poured the juice, pulp and seeds into a strainer she had placed over a small jar.

Then, she pressed them with a spoon to make the juice trickle into the jar. The pulp and seeds left in the strainer were emptied and she started on the next orange half. Eventually, the small jar filled with fresh orange juice. It was then cleanup time. I never knew whether my grandma squeezed her own oranges for economic or nutritional reasons, or both. Perhaps it was due to her love for her family, or maybe it was just out of habit. Whatever the reason, even as a little girl, I remember thinking, that's a lot of work for such a small amount of juice!

Pointer # 2 Determine if the juice is worth the squeeze.

Make a thorough assessment of a situation to ascertain if the process involved justifies the purpose, and the commitment and expenditure of your time and resources.

Stress can be increased by not carefully considering possible alternatives. Shortcuts are great as long as the results you want are not compromised. It helps to learn to work smarter, not harder. After assessment, you may decide to totally abandon an idea. Just be sure the decision is based on feasibility and not fear. The three universal fears are 1) fear of failure, 2) fear of rejection, and 3) fear of confrontation. Yet, in our lives, particularly in the professional arena, we are frequently presented with situations that cause us to experience all three. The expectation of experiencing anything painful generates stress and our state of equilibrium or balance gets threatened. Be willing to ask for help. Through careful assessment you may determine that a team approach will lessen the possibility of failure, rejection, or confrontation and increase the chances for success. If you are not used to asking for the help of others, you'll probably be surprised at how many people are willing to assist, and are also flattered that you recognize their expertise.

Learn to be more proactive and less reactive. Whether done individually, or as part of a team, effective decision-making is empowering and provides a greater sense of control. Below is a method I have devised to aid in making good decisions, thereby reducing stress. Yes, there is a method to my madness! Call this the "I Method."

Identify your goal. What is your purpose? What do you want to achieve? If a problem is confronting you, what resolution do you want?

Ideate. Think about possible routes to your goal and devise a plan to get to each.

Isolate all possible obstacles to each plan under consideration.

Indicate which plan is the most feasible based on the results you want.

Implement your plan.

Inspect the effectiveness of results. Make any necessary changes.

Insure its success by thorough evaluation and follow-up.

This process can be very effectively carried out in the workplace by a team. Team input multiplies the likelihood of success.

The third Pointer comes after this story. I'll never forget Hurricane Opal's visit to Atlanta in October, 1995. Talk about an unwelcome guest! She flashed lightning, roared thunder, and blasted winds all night. Not only was she flashy, loud, and full of air, she left as a thief, literally robbing us of our power. We were without electricity for three days and two nights. I felt rest-broken, frustrated and, yes, "powerless." I tried several times to call Georgia Power. I couldn't get through; all the circuits were busy. No doubt everyone else had the same idea. No TV, no radio, no computer. Plus, the phone went dead and newspaper delivery stopped. My visiting mother, two daughters, and I were cut off from all outside communication. To top it all off we were hungry. I'm a meat & potatoes gal and unless I have a hot meal, I don't think I've had dinner. There we were, lighting our way with candles, and having no means to prepare a hot meal. Needless to say, I was not a happy camper.

The next morning, we were still powerless. I looked out the window and the weather just didn't look that bad. I could not for the life of me understand what was taking Georgia Power so long to restore our electricity. Since we were all hungry, that afternoon, I decided to venture out to buy food, a newspaper and, if possible, a transistor radio. I backed the car out of the garage and drove down the street. I was not prepared for what I saw when I turned the car out of my subdivision. Tree limbs and branches littered lawns and streets; several trees had fallen and one rested precariously on the rooftop of a house. Electrical, telephone and cable wires were mangled on the ground like mounds of spaghetti. It was a disaster area! I couldn't understand it. The view from my window was nothing like this. For the most part, the area outside my window was only lightly disturbed. As I continued driving, slowly weaving around the debris in the road, everything became clear. No wonder we were powerless! I suddenly felt a deep sense of empathy for Georgia Power, accompanied by guilt at how annoyed I'd been with them.

I returned home. Now that I was aware of the magnitude of the situation, rather than wait and whine, I forced myself to really think about how we could better adjust to conditions. I glanced out on the deck and this time I really saw the gas grill complete with cooking jets. It had been there all of the time. With team effort, in no time we were dining on a variety of grilled meats that had begun to thaw, pasta salad, corn on the cob and Texas toast. Now that's my kind of meal! We relaxed on the deck and enjoyed the food and the view.

Pointer #3 Be willing to expand your "view"point.

Recognize when it may be necessary to alter your position in order to promote attitudinal change based on an enhanced perspective.

Realize that your "view"point may be limited or biased. Each of our viewpoints is based on our "window" of experience. We must accept that we are not all looking out of the same window, so naturally we see things differently. Be willing to be more open-minded, less inclined to prejudge people or situations like I prejudged Georgia Power. As we expand our viewpoints, we increase our tolerance and reduce our stress.

This expanded outlook can be very productive. In my professional and personal life, I've been on many teams. One of the most effective and enjoyable professional work teams I've led was one in which each member had uniquely different skills and talents, as well as different viewpoints. The results from the mixing and blending of all those differences were fantastic. We realized great success, not despite our differences, but because of them. Additionally, we each experienced personal growth in the process. Now that's a terrific team!

Adverse situations often cause us to expand our view and to look at things differently. Often, we will find that the answer is right under our noses. Until Hurricane Opal forced me to think outside the box, I had not viewed the gas grill as survival equipment.

My "stormy experience" also serves as a spiritual reminder that in life someone much greater than us knows the big picture. When we don't always understand what is happening or why, there is reassurance that someone greater does.

My fourth, but most important Pointer was also learned from my experience with Hurricane Opal. It made a great impression because it was the first time I had been in darkness for so long. Now, here's "the rest of the story." As I carefully drove and surveyed the extent of damage, I feared we would experience another night of darkness. Then I looked up and spotted several Georgia Power employees working on the lines. My heart soared! Georgia Power was on the job. Light would be restored! But it made me think. Even when I did not see them, Georgia Power was still on the job, just like God is still on the job, even when I sometimes cannot see Him at work during troublesome periods of my life. And, if I could look up and become so excited about Georgia Power, how much more confident and excited I should be to look up to God's Power.

Pointer #4 Look up to your hook-up.

Seek, honor, and stay connected to your spiritual source of power.

In the introduction, I mentioned that a car needs regular realignments for balance. However, a car must first be hooked up to a power source before it will run. I also need a source of power to enable me to successfully move forward. Unlike Georgia Power, only God can rescue me from true darkness. He not only restores the light; He is the light. For my life to be truly balanced, I must remain spiritually connected. We are seeing a resurgence in spirituality as more and more people discover the importance of spiritual connectedness. Their viewpoints change and their lives are enriched as former fears fade. They know that with God as their leader, they are on the winning team. They understand that they must look up to their hook up. Then and only then will success over stress be realized, and success in other areas of life enjoyed.

Success, however, does not usually come in one neat package. Success can mean different things at different ages and stages of life. Our circumstances can alter our message and the meaning of success. I had been happily married for over twenty-four years when my husband, my loving teammate, succumbed to lung cancer. Stress related to loss can be overwhelming. Success for me was to simply feel whole again, to not feel such pain and loneliness. Then God dispatched one of His teams and they went to work. It wasn't a structured or defined team, just a group of people from various walks of life who were all compassionate enough to assume my healing as one of their common goals. I'll forever be grateful! So, for me, success must include my relationship with God and the people He sends into my life during various seasons and for various reasons. A team can help bring you strength, power, effectiveness, comfort and joy; it can help you increase your confidence and lower your stress; it can help you achieve balance and success.

Snowflakes are some of nature's most fragile things,
But just look what they can do when they stick together.
— Vesta M. Kelly

And here's a bonus Pointer: Always remember the importance of humor in your life. To experience the joy of laughter is one of God's great gifts. A popular author has said, "He who laughs lasts." In all areas of your life, surround yourself with a team of positive people, balance responsibility with pleasure and relaxation. Don't allow yourself to become so caught up in the process of living that you forget the purpose of life. Enjoy the beauty life has to offer; occasionally, forget about "dropping the ball," and just have a ball! After all, YOU'RE TOO BLESSED TO BE STRESSED!

ABOUT SANDY POINTER, M.S.W., LCSW

*S*andy *is dedicated to helping people make positive adjustments to life changes, which includes recognizing talents, learning new skills and improving relationships. Clients applaud Sandy's keynotes and workshops on dealing well with personal loss, change, and personal empowerment. She is sought after, too, for staff development training. A popular feature of her work is "Sandy's Pointers."*

A former educator, Sandy has also held positions in administrative and clinical social work. She is the founder of P.A.C.E. (Pointers for Action, Change and Empowerment). Sandy is a member of both the Georgia and National Speakers Associations. She is proud to say she was married for 24 years, is the mother of two talented educators, grandmother to her granddog, Geda, and lives a positive attitude toward widowhood.

Contact Information:
Sandy Pointer, M.S.W., LCSW
P.A.C.E.
3695 Cascade Road
Box 172
Atlanta, GA 30031

Phone: (404) 349-0221
Fax: (404) 349-8602
E-mail: SandysPointers@cs.com

ARE YOU LISTENING FOR THE SOUND OF SUCCESS? IT'S PRONOUNCED TEAM

by Val Jennings

"One of the best ways to persuade others is with your ears — by listening to them."

— Dean Rusk

Shhhhhh! Quiet now! Everyone is talking all at once. Shhhhhhhh! You do not want to miss it: the sound of success. Ah, there it is: it is a team, in full swing tackling the latest project. Who is in charge? Who is saying what? Sound all too familiar?

At some point in our careers, we have or will take part in a team effort toward a common goal. The *value* of teams is undisputed. What is scrutinized is the effectiveness of teams. The most often stated problem with the effectiveness of teams is their frequent inability to complete a project on schedule. An example could be construction projects extending beyond their contractual proposal. Time is not the thief of effectiveness; *listening* is the culprit. It is proactive listening that will deliver the goods: team success.

Before the goods are delivered on proactive listening, it is important to understand the basic growth process of a team to see how proactive listening will assure the successful completion of a project through each level of development. The four stages most commonly identified are forming, storming, norming and performing. A brief description of the four stages follows.

Stage one: forming is the start of the growth process for a team. During this stage, the team participants may be resolving internal issues of their participation (are they a member by will or by assignment?). The question of the purpose of the team comes to the forefront, even if it was stated at its onset, and you may feel alone and isolated in relation to the other team members.

Stage two: storming is typically the most critical time for a team. Members' roles are still vague; territorial issues arise if roles are not defined; abrogation of the leadership ensues if the helm is left unfilled; conflict and eventual dissolution of the team may occur now. Communication is sporadic and often ineffective.

Stage three: norming is the onset of palpable success for the team. Mission, vision, roles and duties are clearer, with the team positioning itself for the last stage. Communication is developing in tandem with the cohesiveness of the team.

Stage four: performing. The essential successful elements of this phase are the collaboration, communication, interdependency and synergy of the group. You can hear the sound of success at this stage: members speak and listen, while effectively and efficiently fulfilling the objectives of the team project.

The first three stages of team growth can be accelerated to the fourth stage by one strategic technique: proactive listening. Success *can* be heard in our teams if we actively listen for it. Just because a team member is speaking does not necessarily mean you are listening to what is being said. Your thoughts may drift to what you are planning for dinner, the next task after this team meeting or even a brilliant reply to what the speaker is addressing. This is not an unusual reaction! Although most of us talk at a rate of 135 to 150 words a minute, most people can think at around 400 words per minute. Some experts claim that it could be as high as 1000 words a minute. This suggests plenty of time to stray from what is being spoken, missing important information that could lead to your success.

In order not to miss even the smallest piece of information, it is important to understand that in every two-way communication, there is a sender and a receiver of information. People tend to speak (send) more and listen (receive) less. We may say that we heard what the other person said (hearing means to "perceive or apprehend by the ear;" listening means to "pay attention to sound — to hear with thoughtful attention").

The critical question is did we *understand* what was said. Understanding requires that we listen proactively and listening *is* a learned skill.

The skill of proactive listening will make you more interesting, more productive and more valuable and effective in your job. In fact, developing the skill of effective listening will enrich every aspect of your life. Active listening is critical when information or direction is given (a report is due by 5:00 p.m.; turn left at the next intersection); when someone is communicating a complaint (your customer is saying that the dry cleaning still has a spot on it); when communicating in a relationship ("I really had a hard day at work"); when making plans with other people (we'll meet Saturday night, instead of Sunday); when entering into contracts and agreements (the house will be painted by the end of the week); when trying to solve a problem through discussion (okay, team members, how will we overcome the shortage of staff?); and when emotional support is needed (tell me about the meeting at school with the counselors).

In these examples, the lack of active listening could produce a lost job (late report); lost time (right turn instead of left); lost business (the customer doesn't come back); lawsuits (the house painting takes two weeks); and overall loss of productivity, profits and impaired relationships. Poor listening habits also form the base of poor morale, misguided management and a drop in employee retention. Studies show that almost all of us listen at a 25 percent efficiency rate. This indicates that we lose three quarters of what is spoken to us. When we listen to ten minutes of information, we remember only about five minutes' worth. Two days later, we remember only about one half of that half, leaving us to remember only about one fourth of what was originally said to us. Simple techniques will enable you to remember more and understand more.

The first technique may appear simplistic, but it is the backbone of the remainder of the skills: **look at the person who is speaking.** So often when someone is speaking to us, our gaze drifts to other people in the room, a quick look at our appointment book or wristwatch, or a glance out a window at the weather. We do look at the person, but often not with the same level of intensity with which the person is speaking to us. The person speaking sees our lack of attention and usually starts to mentally withdraw, leaving the conversation before it is logically finished. We have missed an important moment to communicate to the speaker that we are interested and need the information the speaker is trying to give us. Proactive listening is crucial in the early stages of team development. If all members of your team practiced the learned skills of active listening, the three initial stages of team growth would be shortened dramatically, with success inevitable and swift.

In addition to looking at the person who is speaking, there are other physical cues you can purposely implement that will encourage the speaker to continue to speak, seeing your obvious interest. If you are sitting, lean forward from time to time. It will communicate your active interest and participation in the two-way communication process (as well as keep you more alert). If your speaker says something shocking, respond with appropriate facial expressions (if your team leader has just stated that you are to be the new assistant to the team, this would not be the time to shrug your shoulders and have a blank look on your face). Ask relevant questions of the person speaking. In light of the early stages of team growth, it is essential to understand your role and responsibilities as part of the team. If there were any doubt or confusion, now would be the time to ask questions for clarification ("what will be the scope of responsibilities as Assistant Team Leader?"). This simple step will hasten the growth stage of all members, taking your team quickly to the next level. In addition, verbally react to what the speaker is saying with statements like, "Oh, that's a great idea"; or "I certainly understand what you are saying"; or "that suggestion will work if we can get more support." Verbal reaction gives appropriate feedback to the speaker, letting him/her know that you agree or not or if the information is understood.

Technique number two in proactive listening may, at first, seem difficult, but it is an invaluable skill: **ignore distractions**. You ask, how can this possibly be accomplished? With so much vying for your attention, it is nearly impossible to focus on just one thing at a time. Can you comfortably read a book and understand what is written while waiting in a loud and noisy tire shop for your tire to be changed? Focusing actually takes effort that can measured. When you actively listen, your pulse races, your heart rate increases, and you even perspire. It is possible to become a more effective listener by ignoring distractions. Two steps to accomplishing this are to focus visually and mentally on the speaker and what he or she is saying. While doing this, tell yourself that you will look only at the speaker and that you will hear only what the speaker is saying. Step two is to listen with your eyes. Look for physical cues from your speaker to provide you with more information than what is audible. Wide-open eyes from your team leader may indicate he is surprised about what he is saying. This added piece of information would be picked up only if you were closely listening with your eyes.

Technique number three in the active listening process is to **summarize**. This may seem to be in opposition to the idea of actively listening to each word spoken, taking you away from what is currently happening. Remember: you can think at 400 words per minute, providing time to summarize. When a person begins speaking, it will become apparent if he or she is organized and clear. If the speaker is not organized and clear, rather than become distracted or confused while trying to follow the trains of thought, select main points and key words, forming a short, concise mental summary. Listen for concepts and main idea, rather than facts. If you are able, take notes or make a mental outline of the subject. You can also compare and contrast what the speaker is saying with what you already know. A team example would be the leader of the team saying that being the leader of the team is tantamount to being your boss (when indeed you know another person is your boss).

Summarizing also entails thinking ahead of the speaker. Once you have selected a main idea or concept, think ahead to a conclusion of that thought. If you are right, it will reinforce your memory of what was said. If your prediction is incorrect, the point will be remembered because of its surprise. Mentally travelling in reverse, another tip to summarizing is to review what has been said so far.

The last two aspects of summarization are mentally numbering the points the speaker is covering, and, if you can, create an acronym from key words or ideas (a topic on T.E.A.M., where T = together E = everyone A = achieves R = results).

Technique number four in the proactive listening process is to **tame**

emotions. How quickly we would mentally leave a conversation if the other person were to say that ethnic cleansing is nature's way of controlling population! Shocking! We immediately throw up a barrier, blocking out any information that may further define what the speaker is saying. I am not recommending that you have no reaction at all. An appropriate degree of emotion will enable you to hear sound fundamentals lurking behind the initial statement. Most of us do not have a problem accepting outrageous ideas from people that we know. In light of a team effort, often members come from different divisions or departments of the company. We do not know them very well or just casually, so taming your emotions is crucial to the speedy development of a successful team. By interpreting emotionally charged words before reacting to them, you take charge of the moment, allowing yourself to hear beyond the first words and contemplate the entire meaning behind them.

Technique number five relates closely with number four: **eliminate hasty judgments**. The person speaking to us has a heavy accent, or speaks with a lisp, has a drawl and we are ready to make a hasty judgment. Perhaps your team member has the title of vice president, director or chief. How quickly might you respond to these titles, assigning authority, power, and even fear to what he or she has to say? An easy way to eliminate hasty judgments is to listen with empathy. Opt for the attitude to listen to content, ideas and points of view instead of being blind-sided by impediment, handicap or designation. **Decide** to hear all that the speaker is saying, and avoid selective listening.

Effective listening also entails knowing the difference between connotation and denotation of the words the speaker is using. An easy way to remember the difference is to make a connection with denotation and dictionary — both starting with the letter "D." Denotation is the specific dictionary meaning of a word. Connotation is what a word means through implication and suggestion. A team member may say that the project is very tiring, meaning that it is physically exhausting. You heard the word "tiring" and thought that the team member meant mentally tiring, maybe even boring. To explain further, the 500 most commonly used words in the English language have over 14,000 dictionary meanings. The word "set" has 194 meanings. Can you see where some spoken words could easily be misinterpreted at first blush? Therefore, it is crucial to consider the connotation, the context in which certain words are being used, to understand their full implication. People's experiences, their past, and their knowledge supply connotation, the meaning of the words.

Another aspect to consider when making judgments is whether you are hearing facts or opinions. The words you hear may be charged with emotion, obscuring fact from opinion. A safe way to establish the difference is to ask yourself if what is being said can be verified. An example of this in a team setting would be if the speaker says that the problem being worked on as a team started two months ago. This statement probably can be verified. If the team member says that the problem has caused everyone to become concerned about the future of the company and that the employees are looking for employment elsewhere would present itself as an opinion. Certainly, we can challenge the accuracy of facts and statistics. We simply need to understand the difference between fact and opinion before making a hasty judgment.

Technique number six can be the trickiest. However, if you keep in mind the other techniques mentioned here, you should not have a problem with this point: **Never interrupt**. Your approach to proactive listening should position you to listen to understand. That does not mean simply sitting quietly, uninvolved with what is being spoken to you. There are a number of ways we interrupt when someone is speaking. For example, we can actually speak out while the other person is still speaking; we can mentally argue a point with the speaker; start to deeply consider a point and its ramifications, missing the remainder of what the speaker is saying; we mentally challenge the details of a fact or statistic; disagree with a point the speaker is making; or we don't remain open to further discussion, reason or argument.

This is not a recommendation to provide an intellectual carte blanche to whatever is being presented by the speaker. Your team member may be relating that it is rumored that the project is doomed to failure, and starts to enumerate the many reasons this is so. It would be a natural reaction to **interrupt** with all the reasons you disagree or even agree! However, by listening without interrupting, you may discover that this team member has an inside track with someone in management that has expressed an interest in seeing the failure of this team effort. How critical it is to listen to all of what is said — vital information may just be the last item of what a person is sharing.

When confronted with subjective or questionable information that does not bode well with you, rather than immediately interrupt, quickly ask yourself *Who? What? Where? When? Why? How?* in relation to what has just been said. You will find yourself paying closer attention to the person speaking to see if he or she does indeed answer those questions. If the speaker does answer one or more of those questions, you will probably find that the initial statement is now not so objectionable, having just heard the background, justification or explanation for the subject. Decide on the attitude that you will follow along with the speaker to the end of that thought process. It is amazing that often we discover that another point of view is not only refreshing but may be just the answer we were looking for to complete a task or project.

As equally important as these tips are the main ideas that active listening involves: organizing and analyzing what you have heard; conveying an inclination to listen while not intimidating; understanding the other person's point of view while offering feedback; demonstrating genuine respect for the opinion of the speaker; and realizing that proactive listening reduces communication breakdown while stimulating feelings of worth, understanding and respect.

Using the technique of summarizing along with creating an acronym, the six methods covered here create the word L-I-S-T-E-N. I hope that this tip will make it easy for you in any situation to remember and apply the techniques to assure your success in your professional and personal life. Not unlike riding a bicycle, the more often you ride, the easier and more adept you become. Likewise, with the skill of listening, the more often you apply the techniques outlined here, the more efficient and comfortable you become in their use, with success forthcoming. These six techniques are the keys to rapidly developing a team from its infancy to a mature and "performing" stage. Your listening skills will take your team from forming, to storming, then norming to performing in a short amount of time.

Shhhhhhh! Quiet now! Everyone is talking all at once. Shhhhhhhh! You do not want to miss it: the sound of success. Ah, there it is: it is a team in full swing, tackling the latest project. And proactive listening is the foundation of their success. Are you listening for the sound of success? It is pronounced TEAM.

ABOUT VAL JENNINGS

*V*al *Jennings is a speaker, trainer and coach with over 25 years of training and development experience in manufacturing, healthcare, aviation and academia. Val brings an inspiring history of success in empowering her audiences to explore, discover and implement vital concepts to enhance their professional and personal lives. Her commitment to excellence, drive to succeed and personal philosophy of learning must be enjoyable form the foundation of seminars and workshops that will leave you cheering for more.*

Val is a recipient of the Eckerd 100 Woman Volunteers in America award (1999). She is a member of the National Speakers Association and the Florida Speakers Association. She has reached the highest level of Toastmasters International, Distinguished Toastmaster.

Contact Information:
Val Jennings
Key Concepts, Inc.
P.O. Box 934911
Margate, FL 33093-4911

Phone: (954) 970-0922
Fax: (954) 979-2551
E-mail: Vjennings@Key-Concepts.com
Web: www.Key-Concepts.com

TRUST—THE FOUNDATION OF TEAMWORK

by Pamper Garner

D o you trust your co-workers? Your boss? Would you share your ideas, thoughts or secrets with him or her? Do you feel comfortable exposing the "real you" to the people you work around?

Most people understand the importance of trust to an intimate relationship or a friendship. Trust even has a recognized place in a family relationship. But many people have not thought about the importance of trust in a work environment. After all, we only have to *work* with co-workers — we aren't necessarily their friends. We do not have to trust them. Or do we?

Years ago, my friend was part of a human resource organization at a company when her particular division was merged with two other divisions, both of which had human resource organizations. While all of the detailed decisions were being worked out concerning how to combine the various functions, my friend was busy doing what she had always done — working hard, serving her customers, and doing a great job. She "trusted" that the other people who were working in the other merged divisions were doing the same.

Little did my friend realize that many of her new co-workers were not to be trusted, but instead were acting in very non-trustworthy ways and, in fact, putting her down behind her back.

Unfortunately, my friend's senior management at the time understood nothing about the benefits of having a trusting work place and, in fact, apparently did not care to learn about these benefits. Even though the senior manager spoke of the importance of teamwork (rhetoric in which my friend initially believed), the manager modeled non-trustworthy behavior which certain subordinates copied. The result was that my friend, who had a perfect twenty-year record with this company, was gossiped about, her work was degraded, and ultimately, she was passed over for any of the better jobs resulting from the reorganization.

My friend eventually left the organization, started her own business, and has been very successful. But the experience changed her life and especially her view of trusting organizations.

Unfortunately, as I work with organizations across the nation, stories like this one are prevalent. I hear tales of managers who speak of the importance of working in teams, who apparently have bought into the concept that "two heads are better than one," yet they have no idea how to build a foundation of trust in their organizations so that teamwork can be effective. Many times, while giving lip service to the importance of teamwork, managers are, in fact, guaranteeing that teamwork will *not* be effective in their organizations by their own non-trustworthy actions. That old adage, "Your actions speak so loudly, I can't hear a word you're saying," is still true.

This chapter is about trust as the foundation of teamwork. We will discuss non-trustworthy behaviors, trustworthy behaviors, how our experiences somewhat define our ideas concerning trust, and four steps to take to encourage trust in your workplace.

Definition of Trust

The American College Dictionary defines trust as "(1) reliance on the integrity, justice, etc., of a person, or on some quality or attribute of a thing; confidence; (2) confident expectation of something; hope, (3) that on which one relies."

For purposes of the workplace, I define trust as "a state or condition in which workers and managers do what they say they will do and say what they are going to do in an open, honest, and respectful manner."

Now, you might say, "Well, that sounds good, but how in the world do you apply it in a workplace?" Well, let's look at how to do it.

First Step: What Not To Do

First, you want to ensure that you are not modeling, owning, or allowing any of the following non-trustworthy behaviors.

Top Five Non-Trustworthy Behaviors

As I've traveled around the country doing seminars on this topic, I have asked the attendees to tell me how non-trustworthy people behave in the workplace. The following are the common answers from thousands of workers just like you:

Dishonesty/Lying — These are the folks who simply do not or cannot tell the truth. I once had a boss who was a habitual liar — even when it would have been easy to tell the truth, he lied! What is interesting about this behavior is that it takes only one lie or action of being dishonest for your co-workers to mistrust you.

Several years ago, when my son was much smaller, he had and took the opportunity to tell me a mistruth. Once I found out about it, I told him, "Tyler, if you only knew how long it was going to take for you to earn my trust again, you would never have lied to me." For some time after that, he would ask me, "Mom, do you trust me yet?"

Once someone sees you as dishonest, it takes a very long time for you to regain the trust of that person. So, if you have communicated something to your co-workers or subordinates which has changed or for some reason is now untrue, it is very important that you go back to them and explain what has happened.

Secrecy — This behavior, which I refer to as "playing secret squirrel," is described as withholding information from co-workers, subordinates, or supervisors which would help them be more effective in their jobs. I believe this behavior is based on the adage that "knowledge is power" and the belief that if I know more than you, then somehow it makes me more powerful or more worthy. This behavior is very much a part of the "my turf/your turf" culture we, unfortunately, see in organizations.

Recently, I had an opportunity to work with a higher education organization in planning a civic event. As we talked to this organization's representatives about the facilities they were providing, they would respond to our various requests or questions with statements like "Oh, that's handled by another department — you'll have to call them because we do not talk to them." I was stunned — here we had an organization of higher education which, supposedly, is teaching our students of today how to make a living in the workplace, yet the model the students see is one of departments who do not communicate with each other! Incredible!

"Secret squirrel" behavior will undermine teamwork, and there is no place for this behavior in a team-based environment.

Blaming Others — Have you ever known anyone who cannot accept responsibility for a mistake but, instead, blames everything on someone else? This behavior has been identified as non-trustworthy. Closely related to this behavior are two other non-trustworthy behaviors: paranoia and victimization. Paranoia is defined as behaving as though someone is out to get you. Victimization is described as someone who has a "poor, pitiful me" or "it is just my bad luck" mentality.

People who exhibit these behaviors rarely accept any responsibility for the things that are going wrong in their lives — either personally or at work.

I talked with a gentleman recently who was highly upset about being passed over for a promotion at his place of work. He went on and on about how badly he had been treated, but he never mentioned, not once, his alcohol problem that resulted in numerous absences from work. In fact, the day he talked to me, he had stayed home from work after calling in and telling someone there (not his boss) that he would be there "when he got there."

Now, I understand fully that there are bad companies who mistreat good employees. If you are in one of these organizations, you have at least two choices: (1) stay there, or (2) leave. If you choose to stay, you must accept responsibility for that decision.

If you are one of those people who consistently blames the bad things in your life on someone else, you are not accepting responsibility for yourself, and your behavior is not conducive to good teamwork.

Undependable — The dictionary definition of dependable is "that may be depended on; reliable; trustworthy." One of the key things which tears down teamwork efforts in organizations is people not doing what they say they will do. Over and over, I tell my workshop participants: "To build trust, you must do what you say you will do."

If you don't have the answer to a particular question or problem, say you don't have the answer. If you are still thinking about it, say so. If others are involved in making the decision, say the decision is not completely yours. If you can't say anything about a situation, say so. If you don't know what you are going to do, say so, but whatever you do, once you say you are going to do something, do it. If not, your credibility is undermined and you will not be trusted.

Disrespectful — I recently spoke with a friend who shared with me that she did not feel comfortable expressing her thoughts or ideas to her managers because they might laugh at her or belittle her in some way. She spoke of the importance of treating co-workers with respect and assuring them that their ideas and thoughts are valued in the workplace.

Disrespect is defined as lack of respect or rudeness. If you are treating others in your workplace rudely or disrespectfully, you are definitely not encouraging or enhancing teamwork. Disrespect can be very open or blatant (such as verbal abuse or belittling) or it can be more subtle (such as sending negative signals via body language). Either way, others will typically avoid the disrespectful person or, in a worst case scenario, return the disrespectful attitude, which may result in an open feud. In either case, the effect on teamwork in the organization will be negative.

Second Step: What To Do

Secondly, you want to ensure that you *are* modeling, owning, and allowing the following trustworthy behaviors.

Top Six Trustworthy Behaviors

The following are the top six common trustworthy behaviors provided to me by my class participants.

• *Do What You Say You Will Do* — We discussed this previously, but I want to add that if you cannot do what you said you would do, then communicate this before the fact and explain why. Try to offer an alternative solution, if possible. For example, if you are scheduled to meet someone at 8:00 a.m. and you are not going to be on time, call the person early and let him or her know what time you can make it and ask if that will work for that person. A friend told me recently of having an appointment with someone who was late and did not call until twenty minutes after the appointment to say she was going to be late. My friend said, "I had already figured that out by then!"

• *Openly Share Information and Knowledge* — This simply means sharing important and necessary information freely throughout the organization. And yes, it even means sharing budget and income information.

I recently did some consulting work with a small business which had eight employees. I was hired to facilitate a strategic planning session in which they would identify their short-term and long-term goals for the company. As I worked with the whole group, the camaraderie and high level of teamwork I observed was incredible. Also astounding was the high amount of information that was shared with the whole group. All of the employees were informed as to the current and anticipated revenue. They talked openly about problems and issues, both personal and organizational. There were no secrets! Everyone felt ownership in the business because they were informed! The result was an unbelievably high level of teamwork. You could even feel it in the air!

• *Model Universal Values, i.e., Honesty/Truthfulness/Integrity/Character, Maintaining Confidences* — Have you ever stopped to think about how much our world as we know it depends on everyone's modeling of what I call "universal" values — values that almost everyone agrees on as being necessary to coexist? For example, what if thievery at your area discount or grocery were the rule rather than the exception? What if most people filled their cars with gas and then drove off instead of paying for the gas? What if the norm were to tell lies instead of telling the truth? I think you get my drift. There are thousands and thousands of daily interactions that make up what we humans call "life." The smooth operation of this life is based on the fairly consistent application of these universal values. When others choose to ignore these universal values in living their lives, it complicates life for the rest of us. It is the same with teamwork in an organization. Universal values such as those mentioned here are a very important part of effective teamwork.

• *Be Willing To Do What You Ask of Someone Else* — Nothing promotes teamwork quite like the willingness of team members to roll up their sleeves and get in there and work together on a particular project — no matter what your level.

I once worked with a senior manager who was responsible for a field operation with about six hundred employees who were involved in construction work. I am talking about a man who had responsibility for an 80+ million-dollar budget, but he had an incredible sense of how to build a team and enhance teamwork. In fact, I learned a lot from being a part of this high-performing team, and the experience changed my work life.

One thing I noticed as I traveled with this manager was that when he was around the people who worked for him, he blended in with them; he was like them. He did things his employees were expected to do: He wore safety shoes and a hard hat on the job sites; he arrived early before the shift started; he took the same amount of time they took for lunch, many times eating with them at little roadside restaurants; if his employees worked late, he worked late; if their work was out in the middle of a muddy field, he would tromp through the field with them to see their work.

Is it any wonder that he had employees who would consistently give him and their organization 110 percent? I am talking about unbelievable teamwork!

• *Hold Yourself To A High Standard* — The same manager I mentioned above also always held himself to a high standard. While working with him for a period of several years, I never once saw him do anything that could remotely be considered stretching or breaking the rules. If the speed limit was 55 and he was driving a company car, he drove 55 or less. He did not take the company car out of the way to go somewhere he might want to go.

If you want to enhance teamwork in your team, hold yourself to a high standard. Let others see your high standards.

• *Treat Others Respectfully* — This includes not only treating people with kindness and respect, but listening to them — really listening. Did you know that one of the main barriers to really listening to someone else is thinking about what you are going to say back to that person? We all do this. But it is a barrier to effective listening. Think about your listening habits. Do you often (1) interrupt someone else before they finish speaking, (2) simply not pay attention to what another person is saying, (3) listen for a point of disagreement and then start talking yourself? If so, these are all barriers to effective listening, and you may be treating someone with disrespect just simply by not listening to them!

Another important part of treating others respectfully is to be sure to avoid gossiping. Talking in ways that are meant to hurt someone else's reputation can cause others to see you as vindictive or deceitful, and there is nothing worse for a team than a lot of gossip.

Third Step: Remember The Gray Areas

Well, so far, this is simple enough: You *don't* do the non-trustworthy behaviors and you *do* do the trustworthy behaviors and *presto*! you have created trust in your organization. Well, not quite . . .

When I conduct workshops on this topic, I always give the participants a worksheet that lists fifteen various occupations, and I ask them to rank these occupations in order of trustworthiness. So, they place the number 1 by the occupation they think is the most trustworthy, the number 2 by the second most trustworthy occupation, and so forth.

Usually, "clergymen" as an occupation receives the number 1 from most of the participants. When we discuss the answers, the consensus from the group is usually that clergymen "should" be the most trustworthy, but someone always has a story to tell about a clergyman somewhere who acted in a non-trustworthy way. Many times, that one experience changes the participant's opinion about the trustworthiness of the whole occupation of "clergymen." The class usually has similar discussions about the occupations of judges, psychologists, and physicians. Everyone usually agrees that these occupations "should" be trustworthy because they are positions of trust. However, everyone also agrees that holding a position of trust does not necessarily make someone trustworthy.

The points are: (1) Whether one is trustworthy depends to some extent on the experience of the one doing the judging, and (2) positions of trust are recognized and, to some extent, given credit toward trustworthiness; however, if someone in a position of trust acts in a non-trustworthy manner, the negative effects are substantially more than if that person had not held a position of trust.

So, while much of the topic of trust and trustworthiness appears to be black and white, remember that, in truth, there are gray areas . . . past experiences, individual expectations, and issues related to positional trust.

Fourth Step: Work Hard Daily

I always wonder about a couple on the verge of divorce who, right before the papers are signed, decide they are going to stay together and "try to work on it." I wonder how much they have been "working on it" on a daily basis. And, although I think great extremes should be taken to preserve a marriage, I wonder whether their lack of "working on it" on a daily basis is the reason they are almost in divorce court and whether it might be too late to "work on it."

Working in a team is in some ways the same as working at a marriage. It takes daily perseverance, patience, and nurturing. The time to "work on it" is every day, not after a crisis stage has been reached. One hurtful or careless word or act can bring it all tumbling down, especially if the wrong is never resolved. It's never too late to start "working on it," but it's much easier to be proactive and work on it from the beginning before the black hole is dug too deeply and there is so much baggage weighting you down.

The fact that you have read this chapter indicates that you are interested in a trusting workplace. I hope you will decide to champion the issue of trust on your work team. Good luck!

Trust Quiz

Answer True or False

1. T or F   It is impossible to create trust in your department if your upper management does not exhibit trustworthiness.

2. T or F   To create trust, you must be trustworthy.

3. T or F   As a supervisor, you cannot always tell the truth.

4. T or F   In today's business environment, with all the competition for good workers and business, you cannot create trust. It is just a sign of the times.

5. T or F   In large part, the productivity of your department is dependent on trust and the relationships within the department.

6. T or F   In general, you cannot trust people nowadays.

7. T or F   Upper management, or your supervisor, must be trustworthy before you can be trustworthy.

8. T or F   If you do a good job for the company, you cannot create trust among your department workers.

9. T or F   If you as the supervisor are trustworthy as perceived by your workers, there is a very good chance that your department workers will be trustful of each other.

10. T or F Being trustworthy means being truthful.

11. T or F Being trustworthy means being dependable.

12. T or F Being trustworthy means upper management can trust you to do a good job.

13. T or F Trustworthy, trustful, being trusted, and being trusting mean the same thing.

14. T or F A person who is trustworthy is more trusting of others.

15. T or F Being trustworthy means you have to be naive.

16. T or F Being trustworthy means you have to trust everyone all the time.

If you got:

14-16 correct: Great Job! You understand the concept of trust and trustworthiness as it relates to teamwork in an organization!

10-13 correct: Pretty good, but you need to do some more studying and thinking on this subject.

<10 correct: Too bad! You probably work in an organization where teamwork is nonexistent. Try reading some more on this subject and thinking about what role you might play in promoting a trusting environment in your workplace.

Answers to Trust Quiz

1. F	5. T	9. T	13. F
2. T	6. F	10. T	14. F
3. F	7. F	11. T	15. F
4. F	8. F	12. T	16. F

ABOUT PAMPER GARNER

*P*amper Garner has twenty years of corporate experience and has owned her own speaking, consulting and training firm for seven years. She helps organizations find and implement solutions to challenges in the areas of team building, customer relations and employee development.

Pamper graduated cum laude with a Bachelor's degree in Business Administration from the University of Tennessee. Her professional development has earned her training certificates from Zenger-Miller, Development Dimensions International and Learning International. She is certified to administer the Myers-Briggs Personality Profiles and conduct follow-up workshops. Pamper earned a Bronze Honor Award from the Tennessee Valley Authority for five consecutive years of performance well above standard and was selected to serve on the first Board of Examiners for the Tennessee Quality Award. She serves on several boards of directors in her Chattanooga community.

Contact Information:
Pamper Garner
Pamper Garner & Associates
P.O. Box 390
Chattanooga, TN 37401

Phone: (423) 886-6417
Toll Free: (888) 540-0705
Fax: (423) 886-4602
E-mail: PamperG@aol.com
Web: www.pamperbear.com

WORKING SUCCESSFULLY WITH HARD-TO-LOVE TEAM MEMBERS

by Renee P. Walkup

Whoever came up with the idea of teamwork at work probably never experienced working with the same people I've worked with over the years!

The reality is, we all have to work with people that we can't stand. Every night, you can hope and even pray that the person who is driving you crazy at work will either quit, get fired, or run off to Tahiti. Well, guess what? They *never* do! For some reason, these people stay if for no obvious purpose but to make our lives miserable. (At least that's how it seems sometimes!)

If you are over twenty-one, you've enough experience to know that you can't change people. You also know that you can't run away from every job, every time. The purpose of this chapter is to provide you with some hints, tips, and strategies to work with these difficult people. So before you update your resume, log onto monsterboard.com, or head for your nearest employment agency, let me share with you some experiences I've had with difficult people over the span of seventeen years in the corporate world before I formed my own business. I'll also include some of the strategies that have worked for me as well as others. These ideas, when implemented, should work for you, too!

I'll get you started with a brief profile of some of the most challenging people I've come across — some of whom you are working with, as well. See if one or two look familiar.

First, there was my manager; we'll call him "Jack." Jack hired me into my first management position. Jack and I worked in different cities so my main contact with him was over the telephone. Anytime I called Jack in the mornings to bring him up to date on my region, I was reamed out. It took me awhile, but I finally realized that when Jack's blood sugar was low, he would become irritable, critical, and condescending. He would rant about insignificant work situations, blowing small molehills into colossal mountains.

Then there was Randi. She begged me to come and work for the company that she had recently joined. It looked like a terrific opportunity, but when I arrived, she did everything within her power to undermine me with my colleagues, other employees, and senior management. She even tried to sabotage my position within the company. Since my prayers that she would quit were not answered positively (until the week after I resigned), I had to strategize how to work best with her. This type of back stabber was a detriment to the organization; however, she had the rest of upper management fooled into thinking that she was as great as she professed. Randi wanted to be the fair-haired employee and would go to any length to get to that position.

And how can I ever forget Harold? Harold's ego was so large that his screen saver said, "WHAT ARE YOU GOING TO DO FOR ME, TODAY?" At first, we all thought he was kidding. Then we realized — he wasn't! Harold used to run his meetings literally lying on the floor. He was a bit portly and had a bad back so he justified his lack of professionalism by doing what he wanted — stretching his back. Talk about a lack of eye contact! Harold was only interested in getting what he wanted, when he wanted it.

Then there was the vice president of a software company I worked for, Bruce. This was a person who was so insecure that he would change his mind about a decision at least five or six times before finally signing off on it. All while micromanaging the people involved in implementing the decision! Bruce would get so overwhelmed that he would literally "disappear" within his office and not come out for an entire day. He was totally unavailable. He'd shut his door, turn off his phone, and withdraw from the world. If you tried to speak with him while he was walking out of the building, he would wave you off like a pesky mosquito and say "not now." Bruce clearly had a problem making decisions and sticking to them.

So, how did I manage to succeed in these different environments when I had such dramatic personalities to deal with? More importantly, what tools can *you* use to deal with *your* Jacks, Randis, Harolds, and Bruces? Here are some ideas that you can put to use immediately to make sure you are playing as a team member in your organization without compromising your integrity and professionalism.

If you're working with a "Jack," try to get a better understanding of why he is constantly imitating Oscar the Grouch®. If he seems to get along well with others, but the two of you rub each other wrong, you aren't communicating effectively. Given that you can't change him, consider how you can adjust your own behavior to make your interactions better and reduce your stress level.

Since Jack is a bottom line type of person, begin communicating with him by keeping the end in mind. Bottom line people do not like details, background data, historical information, and, especially, excuses! He just wants the facts, such as when you're going to have a project completed, not the "how"! He is motivated by the *goal*. So, find out his objective — is it to save time, make more money, reduce costs, get promoted, gain attention — you must uncover his bottom line objective and then appeal to *that*. Everything else seems inconsequential and a waste of time for him so it's going to be more challenging for you to get his attention. Have your plan in place before every meeting with Jack. And remember the KISS principle — *Keep it Simple, Sally!*

Here are the six steps to take when dealing with a Jack:

1. Have your plan well thought out
2. Delete the details from your interaction
3. Avoid getting emotional; stick to the facts
4. Ask his/her opinion

5. Keep the interaction fairly brief

6. Get a commitment for buy-in or reach a mutual conclusion

Now you have Randi. Motivated by her own recognition, Randi is a classic case of a two-faced team player. As long as the team members (i.e., management) are important to her to get to where she's going, she plays nice. When she perceives a team member as a possible threat, her verbal arsenal comes out and she attacks. Working with someone like Randi requires full attention to what you say and do around her because she can take an innocent comment, twist it to her advantage, and get you into hot water. Make sure that you are carefully monitoring your behavior and comments when in her presence. Maintaining a professional demeanor and taking the high road is the best way to deal with your co-worker Randi.

However, you must give credit where credit is due. Since she *is* motivated by recognition, it's important that you provide her with a compliment when it is warranted. If this person works *for* you, this is especially critical to your relationship. In fact, Randis are more motivated by recognition than money, so if this is your employee, make sure she is mentioned in the company newsletter and receives written kudos and plaques or other forms of material recognition to get her to continue to play on your team.

Here are the six steps to take when dealing with a Randi:

1. Have a specific plan in place

2. Set a time limit to the meeting

3. Carefully monitor your words and actions

4. Avoid too much intimacy

5. Take careful notes to document the meeting

6. Establish the action that will take place next

Harold is an out-of-the-box type of individual. He moves fast, thinks fast, talks fast, and if you aren't as fast as he is, he will run all over you. (And he'll enjoy the ride!) He searches for weak links in his staff and co-workers and then attacks. This may seem unpredictably cruel to you; however, as long as you understand that he will seek a weakness and play it to his advantage, you can always be prepared for his attack on you.

To work with Harold, you must be on your toes to respond and *quickly*. He is impatient and won't wait for you to formulate your thoughts and calculate your ideas. Also, he is not interested in your feelings, so you must be prepared to keep emotion out of your interactions with him. Have your plan clearly thought out before you talk with Harold about your ideas. Be prepared to keep the thoughts short and with a bottom line result that you can articulate *fast*. Your communication with Harold may end up as a discussion that takes place outside of the restroom over a three-minute period. To you, that interaction was a conversation; to him, it was a strategy meeting!

He'll respect you more if you are really on your toes and refuse to be bullied or pushed around. Stand on your own two feet and never waver on your decisions when working with Harold. Even if you make a mistake later, as Grace Hopper said, "It's easier to apologize than it is to get permission." Especially from someone like Harold!

Here are the six steps to take when dealing with a Harold:

1. Be prepared to have a brief meeting
2. State your facts, fast
3. Avoid getting emotional in the interaction
4. Emphasize what your plan will do for him
5. Take notes on what he commits to
6. Make sure the final outcome is clear to everyone

Now, you have your Bruces to work with. These are extremely complicated individuals because they are warm one minute, cool the next. Their emotions are directly related to the amount of internal stress that they are dealing with. They are totally "me centered," so you may have presented them with a great idea that they loved one day, but two days later, they are rejecting the concept and you are wondering why. Well, the good news is, changing their minds probably had absolutely nothing to do with you! However, many of us tend to take these situations personally.

For example, maybe you have approached Bruce with a terrific plan to increase sales. Bruce asks you some questions, mulls it over in the meeting and acknowledges that it sounds like a solid plan. Now you submit it to him in writing. (Bruces need everything in writing!) You approach him a week later for final approval to implement the plan. He now has another fourteen questions to ask you regarding the plan. You see he is wavering on the decision. Now he is afraid to commit to making this plan happen, even though the end result is to increase sales. How can anyone say "no" to that? Well, it involves change, and this type of individual dislikes change — especially if it involves investing time and/or money. It is too disruptive for the decision maker.

Even though you *thought* you made progress, you ended up just where you began. The strategy to work with Bruce is to have your written plan in place, first. Give it to him *before* you have the meeting. That way, you are giving him time to think over the ideas and to come up with questions before you have your face-to-face meeting. Get the questions from him, in writing, before you meet. That provides you time to prepare by gathering data, researching his questions, and also more time to think of the responses to him. Downplay the idea of "change" and focus on the outcome — all based on research, of course. Since you have already done the majority of your homework, the likelihood of getting a "yes" has been increased dramatically.

Here are the six steps to take when dealing with a Bruce:
1. Prepare, prepare, and prepare for the meeting
2. Make sure you have all anticipated questions ready for a response
3. Have handout materials, back-up data, and copies of all
    documentation ready
4. Bring your notes to the meeting and *take* notes
5. Seek agreement
6. Follow up the meeting with notes in writing

Fortunately for us, not all co-workers are as extreme as the personalities outlined above. Even so, we still have to work with these types and others to achieve results. Since the individuals mentioned earlier are not the most desirable team players, let's take a look at those who are more team-oriented and how they contribute to the success of a team.

The people who are more amiable than those discussed earlier are generally the best team players. Characteristics they exhibit are a willingness to listen to all points of view, an ability to withhold judgement until all sides are heard, and a desire to make decisions based on, not selfish motivations, but the best outcome for the organization. To others, sometimes this person may seem indecisive or weak. The reality is, this person is pliable and often willing to adapt to differing circumstances in a variety of situations. Here's an extreme example of a group of amiable people that you have probably experienced.

Let's say five co-workers are planning on going to lunch. The first one says, "Where do you want to go?" The second says, "Wherever you want to go"; The third says, "I don't care, wherever you guys want," and so on. Until finally someone says, "Well, how about Chinese food?" The next one says, "OK." Another person says, "I'm allergic to Chinese food, but it's ok, if that's where you want to go. I'll find something there to eat — maybe some rice or something." Sound familiar?

These amiable folks may not be the Bill Gates of the world, wanting to own everything, but they are terrific team members — and that often works well when mixed with the Donald Trumps, Bill Gates, and Hillary Clintons in your organization. They are contributing to the team by acting as level-headed facilitators and conduits between the more difficult or challenging team members. The reality is, as a team member you have an obligation to work with all these people. And each person on the team has an obligation to contribute to maintaining a team that works well.

By having a variety of people working on projects together, conflict is almost inevitable. Sometimes, conflict within a team will provide just the energy and emotional enthusiasm that gets people's creative juices flowing. Perhaps in your organization you have an opportunity to influence positive change in the way people work together in their respective teams. For example, you may decide that you want your Harolds and Randis to work together with some of your more diplomatic and confident people. It's important that the latter can't be pushed around, though, because Harold and Randi will want to do just that!

How can these more challenging workers, such as Harold and Randi, transition to become more professional team members? First of all, they need to be made aware that they are an integral part of the team, yet they are not *the* team. Compromise, negotiation, and consensus are critically important to managing a project resulting in a successful outcome. Humor often works, too, in order to get a message across.

Recently, I was at a client's office where a meeting was taking place. This company has an outspoken, pushy person on staff who insists on dominating the sales meetings at this small, successful company. When Robert tried to interrupt one of the owners during his presentation, the owner skillfully said, with a smile, "Robert, you'll need to put another dollar on the table for interrupting." Since we had been laughing earlier about paying a dollar every time Robert used the word "customer" instead of "client," we all laughed and the owner maintained control of the meeting. It also served as a tool to quiet Robert (at least for a while!)

Sometimes it takes the team working together to maintain control, as in that example. If the owner had, instead of using humor to manage the situation, said something like, "Robert, I'm tired of you interrupting all the time. Can't you just wait until I'm finished for a change?" The results of Robert's staying quiet would also have been accomplished, but at what cost? Everyone would have been embarrassed, and the owner would have looked mean-spirited instead of good-natured.

After reading this chapter, are you still hoping and praying that the difficult people in your organization will leave? Well, you're not alone. Just keep trying the hints, tips, and steps provided for you, and you will enjoy a more harmonious and professional team of success!

ABOUT RENEE P. WALKUP

Nationally recognized as an expert in sales and customer communications, Renee Walkup has influenced thousands to make positive changes in their professional lives through her speaking, training and consulting. After 17 years' experience in book publishing, software, hardware and retail, Renee founded SalesPEAK, Inc. in 1996. Among her clients are Coca-Cola, Hewlett Packard, Turner Broadcasting, International Thomson and Outward Bound.

Contact Information:
Renee P. Walkup
SalesPEAK, Inc.
1896 Winchester Trail
Atlanta, GA 30341

Phone: (770) 220-0832
Fax: (770) 220-0833
E-mail: Walkup@SalesPEAK.com
Web: www.SalesPEAK.com

THE KEYS TO A SUCCESSFUL GLOBAL TEAM

by Jane Hight McMurry, M.A.

Eighty percent of the business teams who are successful doing business in their home countries fail when they try to do business abroad. What is the formula for the success of the twenty percent who succeed? The formula's key ingredients include more than product knowledge and hard work. This chapter will unlock the secrets to opening the door to the global business world and provide the keys to success once the team ventures into the world of international trade.

The winning formula results in an essential business tool that gives the team wanting to be successful in the international arena an advantage. This tool is the knowledge of how to deal with people from different cultures. Knowing how to successfully deal with people is vital to dealing successfully in business. The winning formula resulting in this advantage includes three key ingredients: an understanding of the value of cross-cultural training by the entire team, awareness of what every member needs to learn and practice to be an effective member of a successful global team, and realization of the challenges global team members face as they enter the international arena. Cross-cultural understanding is essential to the success of a team conducting business globally.

The Value of Cross-Cultural Understanding

The value of cross-cultural understanding begins with an awareness of the benefits of knowing the correct international style and form. Every member on a winning global business team knows that style and form are closely scrutinized in foreign countries, and they know what that specific style and form are. Teams that create favorable impressions know the code of international business courtesy of the culture in which they seek to do business. Lack of international cultural awareness by just one member is a liability. Business people who are uncomfortable in foreign environments with people who approach business and social interaction from a different perspective are less likely to accomplish their goals. For that reason, the global team seeking success must be equipped with the cross-cultural skills that will enable each member to be calm and confident at all times under all circumstances. To feel at ease with the people they do business with *and* to know how to put others at ease, business people must possess an understanding of the business and social customs of those with whom they wish to do business. The value of knowing the correct international style and form is that businesspeople who hold this key are viewed as leaders and attract others to work with them. Global team building can only then begin.

An important value of understanding the specific culture of an international business partner is that the team will be able to form a business plan with realistic expectations. A carefully constructed business plan that might be tremendously successful in one part of the world can fail miserably if the cultural ways of the people who are involved in the plan are not considered. The team that has an accurate cultural understanding knows the hours of the partnering culture's work week as well as the holidays when businesses are closed. In addition, the savvy team is not only attune to the resources necessary to do business but knows the availability and depth of those resources in the partnering culture. The thwarting of frustration and negative feelings is a further benefit of realistic expectations based on accurate cultural information.

Team building skills for the global team must include cross-cultural protocol to ensure success for two reasons. First, in order for a team to reach synergy, all members must trust each other. Confidence in each other's understanding of the people and culture with whom they are working is vital. Second, the total team's demonstration of cultural understanding through interaction with those from another culture will foster good will, build trust, and establish the foundation for a positive working relationship. The result of this twofold trust is the positioning of every team member to gain better access to people and information which will likely lead to successful business. A polished team that reflects cross-cultural understanding gains trust and respect. People do business with people they trust. The value of establishing trust should never be underestimated. Trust is an important key to global success.

As you can see, knowledge of protocol is valuable to the team that desires to be successful internationally. However, cultural knowledge, product knowledge, and hard work will not make the global team successful without the willingness and ability of each team member to adjust his communication style to successfully conduct business as well as to make and maintain social relationships in a foreign culture. The adjustment of communication style does not mean compromising personal cultural values and traditions. It does mean knowing and showing respect for the customs and traditions of others in order to communicate successfully. The team's global power is significantly increased when every member has the ability and desire to convert cross-cultural knowledge to the team's advantage.

The second key ingredient in the formula for the successful team preparing to do business globally is awareness of what every member needs to learn and practice to be an effective member of a successful global team. Examples follow each key point to illustrate cultural variations.

What Every Team Member Needs to Learn and Practice to be an Effective Member of a Successful Global Team

First, the team member should consider the new international business partner's (ibp's) background. The member will benefit from learning as much as possible about the person with whom he must communicate. Discovery of the age, education, socioeconomic level, etc. of the new ibp will increase the sensitivity of small talk that is necessary for building trust in business and social relationships.

The members of a successful global team should learn key phrases such as hello, please, *and* thank you *in their ibp's native language.* Their interest in polite communication will be appreciated.

The effective team member should know how to greet the ibps correctly. People form first impressions of those they meet within the first thirty seconds. A poor first impression is extremely difficult to change. The savvy international team member knows how to greet the ibp so that the initial impression is favorable. Even though the handshake is commonly used throughout the world, it has variations and is often accompanied by other gestures or greetings. In the United States, the correct business greeting is a firm web to web handshake with two or three pumps accompanied by good eye contact and a pleasant expression. Some cultures offer weak shakes, lengthier handshakes or an entirely different greeting gesture. For example, in Kenya, supporting the right forearm with the left hand is a gesture of respect. In China, the correct greeting is to nod your head; in Japan, the bow is the correct greeting, and eye contact is avoided. The deepness of the bow indicates the social status of the person being met. The deepest bows are for teachers and the elderly. To bow, men place the arms straight down their sides and bend at the waist. Women bow from the waist too, but they place arms straight down and in front of the body. Women position one hand in front of the other so that the hands form a V-shape much like a diver except that the hands for a bow are below the waist instead of above the head. The alert team member takes a cue from the number of bows and the deepness of the bow from the Japanese person. Handshakes are sometimes offered to Americans instead of a bow. The team member can expect a slightly weak Japanese handshake accompanied by a slight bow.

The wise team member knows how to make proper introductions in an international setting. It may be necessary to make introductions at any point during the business deal process. The protocol for the introductions of government officials, military officials, and royalty vary throughout the world. Even in the United States, etiquette for business introductions is different from the etiquette prescribed for social introductions. (Business etiquette is based on rank; social etiquette is based on gender.) In business etiquette, introduce others to the highest ranking business official of the host country. The client is always king. Junior business people are always introduced to senior ranking business people. An easy formula is to say the most important person's name first followed by the phrase "I'd like to introduce to you."

Every team member should know the business card protocol of the ibp's culture. Business cards are an important device for establishing and maintaining contact. Business cards serve as a valuable record of the people met and how to contact them in the future. The Japanese present with both hands, but in the Middle East and parts of Asia the business card is presented with the right hand because the left hand is used for bodily hygiene and is considered unclean. The knowledgeable team member avoids placing the cards in a hip pocket or writing on the card. Every team member doing business internationally has pertinent information printed in his native language on one side and in the ibp's language on the reverse. The quality of the printing is equal to avoid showing deference to one culture over the other.

The effective member knows to emphasize similarities with the new ibp. (Age, family, status, education, sports.) People typically choose to associate with those they perceive as like themselves.

The effective member knows to minimize differences with the new ibp. The member will note obvious differences and adjust verbal and nonverbal styles including clothing style to match the new ibp's.

Every team member should be aware of the ibp's social and political environment. Conversation that will make the ibp uncomfortable is avoided.

The effective team member knows the local public customs and respects them when conducting business in a foreign country. The team member fully understands that in addition to winning points with the ibp, knowing the local ways could prevent personal embarrassment as well as embarrassment to the company, and to the ibp who has begun a relationship with the team member. Further, this knowledge could keep a visitor out of a foreign jail. Americans are not protected by the American judicial system when doing business abroad. Concerns that may seem trivial could cause serious problems if not recognized and respected. For example, the American business woman clad in revealing apparel could get into serious trouble in some foreign lands. In Senegal as in Asia, eye contact is avoided with a person of the opposite sex or who is older or considered higher in status. In the United States, eye contact is expected and the trustworthiness of the person is doubted if eye contact is avoided.

The team members take time to learn the customary business practices of the country they plan to do business with so they will not offend their clients and can get the job done. Moroccans will not do business without the ibp's participation in the customary ritual of drinking mint tea. While Africans in one nation may want to conduct business quickly and efficiently, Africans in other countries, like Mozambique, take a long time as they generally require a stamp of approval from many different people. In China, respect and trust must be earned before the

Chinese will do business. Therefore, close personal ties with Chinese business colleagues must be developed through multiple visits. Doing business in the United States may on the surface seem homogeneous, but rest assured that different businesses have different corporate cultures. In the United States we observe three types of organizational cultures: conservative, modern, and unstructured. The conservative culture may be a banking institution, law firm, or blue chip company like AT&T. It is very structured and has an autocratic style of leadership. Even the clothing is traditional and the atmosphere in the work place is quiet and subdued. The modern culture may be a consulting company or other business that is characterized by team management. The unstructured company is characterized by democratic leadership. The employees tend to be casual and the rules are less defined. The unstructured company may be a new dot.com company housed in a backyard garage.

Every team member should know the correct body language of the ibp and use it appropriately. Adjusting nonverbal communication style to match that of the ibp facilitates communication. To do this, the team member identifies positive and negative nonverbal communication and adopts what is positive in that particular communication culture and casts off nonverbals that are offensive to the new ibp. For example, a person avoids showing the sole of the foot when seated in the presence of those from the Middle East because that body language is considered insulting in that culture. The effective team member knows when conducting business in China that pointing is done with the open hand, not with one finger and that the gesture for beckoning someone is done with the palm facing down and the fingers moving in a scratching motion. In the United States, the gestures of thumbs up or of joining the thumb and forefinger to make a circle (which mean "okay" in America) are acceptable. However, these gestures may have negative connotations in other cultures such as France where this latter signal means "zero" or "worthless" or in places like Brazil, Russia, and Germany where it is the symbol for a very private bodily orifice.

The team member should know the appropriate gift-giving customs of the ibp. In some countries certain types of gifts are expected to express friendship, goodwill, thanks, good luck, or to indicate apology. Not participating in this expected ritual can cause business to fail. The successful team member knows not only the appropriate types of gifts to give and when gifts are expected in the culture of his ibp, but also how to present the gift correctly. For instance, in the Netherlands a gift should never be wrapped. In Japan, the gift-wrapping presentation is more important than the gift.

The effective team member has knowledge of the etiquette of time in the land of his ibp. The etiquette of time is perhaps one of the greatest cross-cultural misunderstandings. Being punctual is very important in many countries and more relaxed in other places. Northern Europe is on time (Germany, Switzerland, Scandinavia, Belgium). Southern Europe and Asia are more relaxed. Respect of time is an indicator of responsibility and trust which are demonstrated by the consistency of team members doing what they say they will do when they say they will do it.

The effective team member knows the approved way to circulate business products among international clients. Some international business has been jeopardized because of ignorance of the approved way to circulate business products among international clients. In the opinion of the ibp, if something as simple as passing an object is not done correctly, more severe errors may follow. The smart team member investigates this area before circulating the team's wares. In Nigeria, for example, objects are passed with the right hand or both hands. The left hand alone is generally thought unclean.

The effective team member knows the dining customs of the client's culture. Business relationships are often forged at the dining table. The team member who fumbles here may erase otherwise brilliant efforts to negotiate a winning deal. The valuable team member knows how to host international guests at a business meal and how to show respect for culinary customs. Islamic law forbids the eating of pork. Some African countries have strict laws regarding alcohol. Chinese dinners are promptly over after the dessert is served. In the United States the tradition is to linger after the meal.

Further, the effective team member knows how to eat a business meal with the appropriate international style. The effective team member in Zaire knows Zairian men and women eat from separate communal bowls and when sharing a dish eat only from the space directly in front of them. Chinese use chopsticks, and Americans may use either the European or American zigzag style of dining. Chinese have courtesies regarding the use of chopsticks, not just the way the chopsticks are held. For instance, it is correct to begin eating only after the host picks up his or her chopsticks. The custom is to eat one dish at a time using the chopsticks and to never touch food with fingers. Some Chinese believe that sticking chopsticks upright in rice brings bad luck — a bad omen for a new business venture. Americans enjoy cuisine from all over the world; however, most regions of the United States have certain specialties and dining styles. It is important to note that while both the American dining style and the European or Continental style of dining are correct, some regions of the United States consider the European style of dining bad manners. Know both styles, observe your host, and be flexible.

The effective team member is sure to know the right way to compliment international business hosts for their generosity. Knowing how to say thank you is a small detail that is extremely important to business success. In Egypt, a guest leaves food on the plate as a symbol that the Egyptian host has provided well. In China, to refuse food is considered rude. If a person doesn't want to eat a particular item, it may be removed to the side of his dish. To eat rice, the diner brings the bowl to the mouth, and shovels the rice in with chopsticks. In the United States, the effective team member accepts a portion of all food offered by the host for the meal and takes at least one bite of each food.

The effective team member knows the business days and non-working holidays of the international client. This information may save time, frustration, and money. The savvy team member in South Africa knows that the country is comprised of numerous ethnic groups practicing different religions and observing different non-business holidays. The savvy team member in China knows that one of the biggest holidays in China is the celebration of Chinese New Year which is also called Spring Festival. The date is based on the Chinese lunar calendar. In the United States, American businesses are often closed on holidays unique to Americans. For example, the fourth Thursday in November is the American Thanksgiving. Some presidents' birthdays have been designated as holidays when many businesses are closed. Consult the company you want to visit before you arrive.

Challenges Global Team Members Face in the International Arena

Now that the value of cross-cultural understanding and what every team member needs to consider in order to be effective in international business relationships have been discussed, I would like to conclude by providing a final key ingredient to the winning formula — the importance of realizing the challenges global team members face as they enter the international arena. The team member who takes the easy path believing that one's own culture is best and that an attempt to understand a different culture is not important will likely be taken off guard, feel foolish, flounder in the international marketplace, and spoil not only the chance at personal business success, but also that of the team. The following information is provided in order to create an awareness on the part of the members of the team in hopes that members will be spared undue anxiety throughout the process of conducting business as part of a global team and that success in the global marketplace will be their reward.

First, they are challenged to be open to other customs of doing business and challenged to be patient with people who lack understanding of other cultures and knowledge of international protocol. Second, international business people are challenged to conduct business using the correct protocol as well as good manners. Manners are how we treat other people. Protocol refers to the formal written code of interpersonal communication. It is not a modern concept. It has long been the grease for positive human interaction used effectively by successful people for centuries. The best way to treat others was written long ago and is known as The Golden Rule, "Do unto others as you would have them do unto you." In the international arena, the "The Platinum Rule" may be even better, "Do unto others what they would like you to do." This applies as much in written and nonverbal communication as it does to verbal and face-to-face communication. The third challenge for business people is to take the time to learn and to understand the regional customs of their own culture as well as the customs and courtesies of the countries in which they seek to do business. And finally, business people are challenged to accept the view that the customs and courtesies of one country are no better that that of another — they are merely different.

Truly knowing how to get along with others and to communicate effectively is a skill that can make or break relationships and careers. International cultures, like international foods, add an intoxicating flavor to life. Customers return to international restaurants that have good food and they return to do business with international business teams that have good international people skills. But the modern business person who takes the time to unlock the secrets of cross-cultural communication will gain something even more important than a new or extended business contract. He will gain self-respect, and that is more important than riches or fame, for self-respect is the only thing that brings true happiness. Remember the words of the prophet, "He who respects himself will earn the respect of all the world." Of all the keys of which I have written, that is the key with the notches that will open the world of happiness.

"To establish oneself in the world, one does all one can to seem established there already."

— LaRochefoucauld

ABOUT JANE HIGHT MCMURRY, M.A.

J ane Hight McMurry is a world-class communication and etiquette expert. She teaches professionals how to succeed in the personal areas of business. Her presentations are creative, include unforgettable visuals and are designed to entertain while revealing the secrets of American and international communication.

Jane studied at Oxford University in England and graduated Phi Beta Kappa from the University of North Carolina (Chapel Hill) with a Master's Degree in Communication Studies. Her company, The Etiquette Advantage (TEA), presents up-to-date and well researched American and international business communication skills. One way Jane stays current on emerging trends is through memberships in the American Society of Training and Development, North Carolina World Trade Association, New York Council of Protocol Executives and the National Speakers Association.

Contact Information:
Jane Hight McMurry
The Etiquette Advantage
P.O. Box 4544
Wilmington, NC 28406

Phone: (910) 762-0703
Toll free: (800) 782-2443-12
Fax: (910) 762-0703
E-mail: EtqAd@aol.com
Web: IntBusCom@aol.com

THE FIVE DISTINGUISHING CHARACTERISTICS OF MEMBERS OF EXCEPTIONAL TEAMS

by Marie Benoit, Ph.D.

Some of my most painful childhood memories immediately come to mind whenever the topic of "teams" is mentioned. You see, I am one of the most "un-athletic" individuals you will ever meet — and as a child, I was even more "un-athletic" than I am today. I still cringe when I think about my experiences in physical education class. I remember as though it were yesterday the horror I felt each time I heard our physical education teacher shout, "Select your teams!"

Surely, you all remember what that was like. Everyone lined up in the middle of the gym floor as though ready to face the firing squad (which is exactly what this felt like to me). The team captains stood before us and one by one they selected those individuals most likely to enable their team to win. At first, selections were made very quickly. But once all the "good" players had been taken, the process slowed considerably. As I recall, this is the part that seemed to last an eternity. Invariably, there were a handful of students still standing, students that neither captain wanted. Both captains knew, however, that they had to continue selecting until all students were on a team. So while the whole class watched, they slowly divvied up the remaining few. As you have probably guessed, I was always one of the last chosen. It was humiliating!

All of these years later, I know that regardless of the type of team — a sports team, an association of business executives, a family, a civic organization, or a department at work — sometimes members are hand-picked by the team leader and sometimes they are members by default. In either case, the team's strength, or weakness, is dependent upon its members. Think for a moment about a team that you have been a part of that was truly an exceptional team. Contrast that exceptional team with one from your past that was not-so-exceptional. What are the differences in the two?

I believe people make the difference. As I have analyzed various types of teams and discussed this topic in team building sessions over the years, I have found certain characteristics to be present in members of exceptional teams. I believe these traits will be even more important to teams as our already fast-paced society becomes more and more technology dependent and moves at even greater speeds. Whether you are a team leader choosing members for your team or a team member who wants to be the best member you can be, here are the characteristics that I believe are found within individuals who make up exceptional teams.

C - Committed

A - Achievement-oriented

R - Respectful

E - Expressive

Committed

Dedicated or pledged to support a belief or cause

Members of exceptional teams are committed to doing their absolute best. Unlike so many people who proclaim to do their best each day, they can look themselves in the mirror every morning and say, "I did my very best yesterday and I will do my very best today"— and really mean what they are saying. They have a commitment to themselves to do the best they can do.

We all know, though, that even when someone does his best,

another person could come along and do the same thing even better. People have varying levels of ability. Some people have more skill and talent in some areas than others. An exceptional team, therefore, realizes that each member has something to contribute and determines what strengths each person brings to the group. A member's responsibility to the team then becomes something in which he excels, something in which he already has a strong commitment to succeed.

An exceptional team is comprised of a group of members who are "experts." These team experts realize that each is part of a whole. Without the contribution of each, the group will not function properly and will not be able to adequately accomplish its mission.

Each member is, therefore, committed to his role for the good of the team.

Achievement-Oriented
Desire to accomplish, to gain or reach by effort

Members of exceptional teams have a strong desire to achieve their goals. They are usually very busy people who are exceptionally well-organized — not necessarily in the sense that everything around them or about them is in order, but that everything in which they are involved gets done on time.

Time, to achievement-oriented individuals, is extremely precious. They realize more than others that what we waste of it, we can never regain. While we are each given the same number of hours to use every day, they accomplish much more than the average person in that twenty-four hours. How do they do it? I believe the secret is planning.

By planning, you save time. For example, you will save time in the morning if you plan what you are going to wear the night before. You will save time at the grocery store if you plan what you need to buy before-hand. You will save time on a trip if you plan the best route to take before you leave. You will save time in a meeting if there is an agenda. The more time you save, the more time you have to get more done — or the more time you have to put "quality" into what you already are doing.

By planning, you know where you are headed. As Zig Ziglar says, "How can you hit a target that you cannot see? Or better yet, how can you hit a target that you do not even have?" Achievement-oriented people accomplish more because they set goals, put those goals in writing, come up with plans for accomplishing those goals, and follow through with those plans.

Achievement-oriented team members are planners who not only get things done but get them done right and on time. They keep their eyes on the ball — or the team's goal — and keep the team moving in the direction of accomplishing that goal.

Respectful

Showing attention or consideration

Members of exceptional teams are respectful of others. They are genuinely nice people, the kind of people that everyone likes being around. They are considerate of your time. When a respectful person tells you that he will be there at 10:00 a.m., he will be there at 10:00 a.m. — or he will call to let you know that he will be late. He will only be late, however, because of situations beyond his control. Except perhaps when a flight is delayed or traffic is at a standstill, this person will be there on time every time. You can count on it.

A respectful person is one that you can depend on to get the job done. Not only will the job be done, but it will be done better than you expected. For example, he will not only be prepared to give an oral report, but will also have a written report. Not only will there be a written report for you, but copies for everyone else involved. A respectful person goes beyond what is expected.

A respectful person takes full responsibility. Once the job has been assigned to him, he takes ownership. He needs no supervision. He will figure out how it needs to be done. He will find the appropriate people, if necessary, to help him get things done. "Whatever it takes" is his attitude.

A respectful person is honest. If he knows he cannot complete a task by the date you are suggesting, he will tell you — rather than have you believe that your deadline is possible, only to find out later that it cannot happen by then. He will offer alternatives that may be helpful to you. Even if it means giving up your project (which would mean money in his pocket), he would rather recommend someone else who may be able to do the project for you than accept it and not be able to do it well and by the deadline. In the long run, honesty is still the best policy.

Expressive
To communicate or make known one's thoughts or feelings

Members of exceptional teams are willing to express their views. They understand the importance of communicating with the rest of the team. They know that people are not mind readers and that the only way others will know their points of view is to share them.

Sharing ideas, thoughts and feelings is an excellent vehicle for determining new strategies for accomplishing the team's goal. All of us have ideas within us. Sometimes, however, those ideas remain within unless we are willing to take a risk and "go out on a limb." Exceptional team members speak up even though doing so may sometimes make them feel vulnerable. They let the team know why they may disagree with a specific procedure or concept; they offer alternative solutions. They also listen objectively to the ideas of others. Only when members express their views in this way can the team grow beyond its present state. Being expressive stimulates team creativity; creativity produces new and better ways for accomplishing a team's goals. Being expressive is good for the team.

Caring

To feel concern or interest, to feel affection or liking

The "golden" thread that binds the members of an exceptional team is that they care. They care enough to be committed — to themselves to do the best job possible, to the role they play as a team member, and to their teammates. They care enough to want to achieve as much as possible every day, for themselves and for the team, and they set goals in order to make that happen. They care enough to respect themselves and are respectful of others as well. They care enough about themselves to know what they have to say is important and perhaps beneficial to the team; they, therefore, express their views and are careful to listen objectively to the views of others.

Members of exceptional teams are caring individuals. They are the kind of people who always make us feel good. In fact, they can find "the good" in everyone and they go out of their way to do so. Caring individuals compliment you when you deserve a compliment. While these individuals generally give more compliments than others, it is important to note that the compliments are well-deserved. Caring individuals are always very sincere and give a compliment only when there is something to compliment.

Caring individuals also express their appreciation when you have done something that in some way affects them. Their words are sometimes verbally expressed but more often are said in conjunction with a handwritten thank-you note. Depending on the deed, you may also receive flowers or a gift basket in appreciation. They send letters to your association or boss or spouse commending you for the job that you did for them. They may even send recommendation letters to friends and colleagues who may be able to use your service. The point is these people care enough to take the time to let you know how much what you did really means to them.

Caring individuals also want to know whether they are giving you the best treatment possible. Therefore, periodically they will sit down with you and ask, "How can I do a better job of serving you?" A caring person will then do more of all of the things you indicated he does well; likewise, he will do better at all of the things that you mentioned could be improved. The key point here is that this person cares enough about your relationship to ask.

Caring individuals think about you when they read an article they think would be of interest to you. But unlike many of us, they take the next step. They photocopy the article, address an envelope, put a stamp on it, and actually mail it! They are thoughtful, kind people who take the time to do a little something extra for you.

When you can find an individual who is committed, achievement-oriented, respectful, expressive and caring, you have found a remarkable person. When you can find a team comprised of a whole group of individuals who are committed, achievement-oriented, respectful, expressive and caring, you have found an exceptional team—one that is capable of excelling in every area it sets out to conquer. If your task at hand is to handpick your team members, may you find individuals who possess these characteristics. If you are a team member seeking to be the best team member you can be, may you concentrate on incorporating these traits into your character and sharing their importance with your team.

I cannot help but wonder whether I would have been less traumatized as a child had our physical education class had an introductory lesson on team building prior to the time teams were first selected. What if we had understood that all students had something to contribute to the team? What if we had realized that not only did the team need members who could hit the ball, catch the ball, and run — but members who could call the game, maintain the equipment, keep the score, etc. — and that every role was important? If I had been selected as the team's scorekeeper because of my attention to detail and reputation for accuracy, would I and others have felt that my role was as important as

catching, hitting, and running with the ball? Would I have been committed to my role as scorekeeper had I been taught that each team
member's role is a part of the whole and that it takes all of us working
together for the team to achieve its goal? If we had learned about the
importance of expressing appreciation to each other, would I have been
motivated to do an even better job? While we will never know for sure,
I cannot help but think that such a lesson on team building could have
made a tremendous difference during a difficult period in my life. I
believe it could quite possibly make a difference in the lives of many
children — and perhaps some adults — today. If you agree, I urge you
to share this chapter with others.

ABOUT MARIE BENOIT, PH.D.

*D*r. Marie Benoit has been an educator for over 25 years. She began her teaching career in 1975 after receiving a B.S. in Business and Office Education from Northwestern State University (LA). After obtaining a master's degree in Business, she taught at the College of Business at McNeese State University. In nine years she progressed from Instructor to Associate Professor. She earned her Ph.D. from North Texas State University in Business/Communications.

In 1985, Dr. Benoit left her tenured university teaching position to found the Business Enhancement Institute. She leads seminars for business leaders. Her most popular topics are: presentation skills, conflict resolution, time management, organization skills, team building, customer service and dealing with change. Her specialty is working closely with presidents, CEOs, entrepreneurs and senior management leaders.

Contact Information:
Marie Benoit, Ph.D.
Business Enhancement Institute
9622 Ridge Ave.
Fairfax, VA 22030

Phone: (703) 267-5650
Fax: (703) 267-6651
E-mail: MBenoit@erols.com

Can't Get No Satisfaction!. . . Want A Better Way?

by Tom Guzzardo

B ob was checking his voice mail from his car Friday morning as he was stuck in traffic at 7:21 on a beautiful spring day. He had canceled an 8:30 a.m. marketing meeting with his staff in order to meet with one of his biggest clients. His greatest fears were coming true. He had back-to-back meetings with clients at 8:30 a.m., 10:30 a.m., 2 p.m., and 4 p.m. His voice mail message said that two of the proposals he was making to clients that afternoon were not ready yet because of computer problems. As his frustration was building, he thought, "Why do I even pay these people? This teamwork thing is not working." At 5:30 p.m., he was supposed to pick up his daughter and take her to soccer practice, then rush home to cook supper at 7:15 p.m. because his wife would be working that night.

The New Partnership Paradigm

We live in a time of rapid change, high stress, and increased demands to be productive, focused and efficient. As we enter the new millennium, we are called to work together in teams and to partner with the people with whom we work and live. We all understand the power and potential of effective teams. We've had glimpses of the synergy and power of teams as we have had great experiences of being part of a winning team in sports or in community projects.

We also know the frustration of having a group of talented people but no cohesiveness within the group. We can tap into the group's potential if we identify what is missing within the team process. The distinction of what is missing becomes clear once we identify old and new paradigms of doing business. The old paradigm is characterized by hierarchy and structured environment. The concept here is productivity and product rather than people. People in this paradigm are very comfortable with a structured environment with defined lines of authority.

The new paradigm is characterized by partnership. The people working within this model want authority and responsibility. They are not comfortable blindly accepting authority. They need to feel that their contribution is valued and important to the company's success. They need to feel something is at stake. If they don't feel that their contribution is necessary, they will move to a place where they will be valued, necessary and respected.

Hierarchy Paradigm		Partnering Paradigm	
Decision making:	top down	*Decision making:*	unilateral
Information:	limited, held at top		available and broadly understood
Communication:	one-way	*Communication:*	two-way
Rewards:	high at top low at bottom	*Rewards:*	available to all proportionate to level of responsibility
Responsiveness:	slow and reactive	*Responsiveness:*	immediate and proactive

The challenge in the workforce is that there are two paradigms that are mutually exclusive and incompatible. A new set of skills and attitudes are necessary in the new millennium to effectively create a new paradigm for doing business which generates partnerships and has results flow from that relatedness. A key distinction for building winning teams is the ability to have partnership coaching. Partnership coaching is a leadership skill in which all of the players are able to give and receive feedback. The players believe that they fully contribute and have a stake in the future success of their company.

Creating effective teams in today's business world can be achieved only through partnership and relatedness. Instituting the team-building process involves the following steps:

1. Gather Information — Ask questions, listen and explore until you come to clarity about the real problem, issue and need at hand.

2. Gain Understanding — Keep the conversation moving until you have a new idea that works for the new solution that everyone can agree upon or an "aha" solution about the problem being explored. With new understanding about the problem, the team quickly finds a new solution that builds synergy and the team runs on its own.

3. Take Action — After there has been a consensus and an "aha," it's time for action. New solutions, new ideas and new strategies are set up and acted on with solid commitment and enrollment.

To be effective at this team leadership/partnership process, we need to learn the skills of coaching. Coaching is being able to give and receive new ideas, support, and authentic feedback. Coaching is a process of teaching, facilitating and empowering people to expand their visions of themselves and their life situations. Coaching helps people to transform their attitudes, skills and strategies to be more productive and to be related to each other.

It is important to understand in the team-building process that everyone is a coach and everyone is constantly being coached in our new, interconnected world community. Whenever we are giving and receiving feedback, or negotiating a new idea or need, we are coaching each other.

Partnership coaching takes new skills, listening from the heart, and co-creating solutions and ideas. To be an effective coach, one must be patient, receptive, serving and caring.

Partnership Coaching is Characterized By

1. Caring: an attitude of genuine concern, respect and acceptance of support, being willing to actively help others achieve their goals and intended results

2. Support: the actions necessary to help another achieve the key objectives and help develop the potential of others

3. Acknowledgment: giving genuine thanks and appreciation for others' contribution and help.

Here is an actual case of a company that I have been coaching on team building. Bob is a 47-year-old entrepreneurial business owner. He is the father of two teenage daughters, a baby boomer, a former college football player and leader in his community and church. He runs a sales and marketing firm which has twenty-five employees. He and his company are a good prototype for all of us caught between the old model of doing business focused on authority-based, top down strategies and the new business model of shared authority and responsibility, partnering and team building. As we observe a week in the life of Bob and his company, we will share the events and story and periodically step back to examine what's happening and the lessons for Bob and his people along with ourselves. Let's join the story in progress.

Scruggs Team Story:
Breakdown with Chuck and Karen

It's now 10:25 Friday morning, and Bob is walking out with his client, having completed a productive meeting. Bob shakes hands with the client; they both smile and agree to touch base next week.

Bob walks briskly into Chuck, Operations Manager, and Karen, Office Manager, and asks if the proposals are ready for his 10:30, 2:00, and 4:00 meetings. Chuck and Karen look up in panic. Chuck says, "We had computer problems yesterday, Bob. The 10:30 proposal we are printing right now and we have halfway finished the 2:00 and 4:00 proposals as we speak.

Bob says, "Chuck I've got to have this stuff. Why haven't you got this stuff to me sooner?"

Chuck retorts, "Bob we just got these three requests for proposals two days ago! And we've had computer problems."

Karen says, "Also, Bob, in working with the proposals we were unclear on your real outcome and the strategies you wanted us to amplify on the proposals."

Bob says, "This is ridiculous — the information I gave you was very clear and my requests are equally clear."

Chuck replies, "Bob you have been running so hard you haven't slowed down to talk to us, and we don't know what you want. We are trying to help you." Bob glares at Chuck and says, "this isn't my idea of really helping." Karen says, "Bob how can we help you now?" Bob says, "Get the proposals to me and stop giving a lot of excuses. Karen, we've got to review my schedule of appointments for the week."

Let's step back and see what we can learn from this situation so far. I think we can all relate to rushing to meet last-minute deadlines and dealing with breakdowns. My definition of breakdowns is *any situation in which we are not getting our planned desired results.* In Bob's coaching of Chuck and Karen, what was missing? Did he create rapport? No. Did he discover the real problem and issues blocking his getting his proposals? No. When he was confronted with a breakdown, he became frustrated, blamed other people and didn't find out effectively what the real problems and issues are. Admittedly, there wasn't much time to do that. Did he do good performance coaching, i.e., stating his desired outcomes and the actions that he needed to his objective? He made requests but in a judgmental, critical fashion. Did they agree on a clear action plan and accountability on what would be done by when? Not really. They were simply reactive and trying to survive the breakdown.

If Bob, Chuck and Karen are wise, when things calm down, they will critique the situation and discover what they need to learn. Great coaching happens when we ask, "What do we need to learn? Do we need to change our system of communication? Change our sales/marketing proposal process?" Let me ask you, "What coaching needs to occur with Bob and his people to improve their teamwork and communication? What does Bob need to do differently to be an effective coach?" Let's return to our story.

Bob's Team Meeting

Chuck and the marketing and sales support people scramble to get Bob ready for his remaining appointments Friday, and the proposals are handed to Bob at the last minute. Luckily his clients for the 2:00 meeting were late and the 4:00 meeting people were gracious as the meeting started fifteen minutes late. The next work day, Monday at 9:00 a.m.,

Bob met with his entire team to have their weekly staff meeting. They went over the key goals for sales, marketing, customer service and operations. All the key departments were represented. As they followed a clear agenda, they were rushing because Bob had a client appointment scheduled for 10:00 that morning. Though Chuck was the team leader/coach and meeting facilitator, Bob interrupted a number of times and rushed things along as he talked to his key department heads.

Bob stated, "Karen, you need to be more on top of my schedule; you're scheduling me in too tight. Here are the people that I need to see in the next two weeks. Please make sure that these appointments are set up with clients and these key vendors."

Karen responded, "Bob, there are only five remaining time slots in the next two weeks and you want me to schedule seven clients and three vendors. I need you to open some time slots in your schedule or get with me."

Bob said, "Look I am running to a meeting. I will be in meetings all day; open up some time on Tuesday or Thursday mornings."

Karen replied, "Tuesday morning you blocked to go to your daughter's school play, so that is not available."

Bob said, "Fine — whatever — catch me in the car between appointments."

She said, "I have a couple more questions."

He said, "I will have to talk to you later; we've got to move on."

Bob rushed through his instructions with the customer service team and with marketing on what he wanted for the week. There was little time for their questions and requests on the projects that they were working on and the upcoming marketing client appreciation seminar in three weeks. Then Bob told all of the key managers and department heads that he needed them to hand in their quarterly project goal report sheets a week early. They resisted his request and ideas. He also dictated that he wanted their weekly management activity tracking sheets to be done in a new format with more detail and to be on his desk every week by Friday morning, not Monday morning. This was met with more resistance; again Bob minimized the questions and discussion. At the end of the meeting the tension and stress level in the room were really high. One of the managers mumbled on his way out, "This teamwork and two-way communication really works great."

What just happened? In Bob's interaction with Karen, his office manager, he was rushed and was in a *telling* mode as opposed to a *making requests* mode. In his coaching her, he was pushed for his results and was eager to get things done. There wasn't much two-way communication. Bob created some rapport but never really discovered or heard her needs or concerns. As he made his request, his desired outcomes were clear, but the actions he suggested to solve the problem and schedule the clients, vendors and business coach were not effective and focused. As it did turn out, when she tried to catch him the rest of that day and the next day, he was out on appointments and did not respond to her voice mail in the midst of his busy days. I find many busy managers, leaders and people today are running really hard, but they are not able to create two-way communication and give and receive support to effectively reach their goals. It is very easy to get into a telling, assertive mode as opposed to co-creating a solution and developing the mutual support necessary to achieve the desired results.

Bob came up with some productive strategies on his own to create more accountability and feedback from his managers on their projects. He did not get any management staff feedback on how these changes would impact the needs, goals and deadlines of his key department heads. Thus he did not create good rapport, and he demanded that his needs be met. He is not able to do effective performance coaching to mutually create desired outcomes, actions, and reports in a way that would be a win both for him and his department heads. Thus there was a high degree of tension and frustration. Our challenge is to slow down and take the time necessary to co-create solutions, systems and strategies that are a win for all of the people involved. Do we take enough time to enroll the people around us in supporting us? Do we listen enough to what their needs are as we look at setting up new goals, new plans, and new work processes? In the midst of going for top results, do we leave out the relationship and the relatedness?

Chuck Calls Tom for Support

Tuesday afternoon at 4:30 p.m. Chuck called me for support.

"Tom, we need your help. We are experiencing a major breakdown: Bob is barking out orders, not listening to our contributions. He changed a major procedure without getting our input and everyone's frustrated."

Tom identified the breakdown as the absence of partnership coaching. Bob, like most top managers in a hierarchy paradigm, goes straight to action. Then everybody becomes frustrated because the team process does not come to fruition.

"Chuck, you've got to do partnership coaching to help him see what's missing. Coach Bob on the four steps in partnership coaching":

1. Create RAPPORT with him: be in his world, see things from his side, slow him down.

2. DISCOVER the NEED OR ISSUE going on with Bob. What's he trying to accomplish? What's he afraid of? What's driving him?

3. You've got to do *PERFORMANCE COACHING AND TRAINING* with him, helping him to see what's missing in the way he's coaching and doing the team process.

4. Then set up an *ACTION PLAN* with him on what he needs to do and create accountability, support and follow-up.

Tom said, "You started well in the process by having a team meeting, but Bob didn't gather information and clarify the real problems with you guys. Then you guys didn't discuss and keep talking until you came to the insight, the 'aha!' the true understanding. Chuck, remember that coaching goes both ways as you co-create solutions. Bob is so focused on production and results that he is missing the people and forgetting the process. Chuck, you and Bob need to understand what is truly going on with your people and what needs to happen to perfect your work processes."

"That makes good sense. I need to meet with Bob. I'll send him an e-mail and request a meeting with him early tomorrow morning. Thanks."

What's going on: Tom gave Chuck good support by hearing his frustration and issues. They agreed to both e-mail Bob and give him supportive feedback on where things are breaking down and make a request that Chuck and Bob schedule a time to talk in the next twenty-four hours. Chuck and Tom were able to look at where there was a breakdown in following the team guidelines of speaking the total truth with caring, listening from the heart, and attacking the problems, not the people. They also looked at practical ways Chuck could coach and confront Bob in a way that would be supportive and proactive. Chuck and I were able to come up with a strategy to create a two-way dialogue with Bob. They worked on setting up a communication system that had been breaking down between Bob and Karen and his other key department heads.

The challenge for all of us in the midst of breakdowns and heavy pressures and deadlines is to stay calm, re-focus and ask ourselves, "What do I need to learn?" "What do we need to do differently?" We need to set a new action plan, and be accountable and take action. We can expect breakdowns, but can we co-create new solutions and systems? Can we create new results and relatedness?

Bob and Chuck Clear the Air

Back to our story . . . Bob received constructive e-mails from both Tom and Chuck giving him feedback about the current situation and the breakdowns. Bob needs time to read the e-mails and reflect. Bob caught Chuck in the hall early the next morning at 7:40. He smiled at Chuck and said, "I guess we need to talk. It seems like I've been running really hard. Sounds like the management team is really frustrated about my new accountability and reporting system, huh?"

Chuck smiled and said, "Yeah, we need to coordinate a little better. I understand that you are running hard and stressed."

Bob scratched his head and said, "Let's step back and see what we need to do."

The two men discussed ways to better coordinate Bob's schedule. They co-created a solution to have Bob have a detailed schedule eight weeks ahead, blocking out time for sales appointments, marketing appointments, team staff meetings, R&D, building strong client centers of influence and more buffer time. They also agreed that Bob would need to personally clean things up with Karen and hear her needs and frustrations and spend some quality time together. Bob and Chuck brainstormed ways to get the management team on the same page as far as giving Bob more feedback on the key projects that people are working on. Bob and Chuck agreed to work on their total quality process for value-added follow up with their top fifty clients. They both agreed that Bob would have a mini-team-meeting with the four senior department managers, one-on-one over the next two days. Bob was to enlist their feedback on how to create good management reports in a way that would be effective for both Bob and the department heads. At the end of the meeting Bob said, "I thought I was being effective and reasonable; I guess I have a tendency when under pressure to isolate and give orders rather than give and receive support from my team and the people that really care about me and the company."

What was learned: Bob was able to quickly create rapport with Chuck by being humble and real, by being authentic and genuine about his mistakes and the pressure that he was feeling. As Bob was calmer, accepting and affirming, they were able to discover the problem areas and concerns that needed to be addressed. Next they were able to do some excellent performance coaching and training on dealing with the problems at hand — setting very specific strategies on how to set up a better system, scheduling events with Karen and cleaning things up with her. They also co-created some practical actions and solutions to enroll the management team on giving Bob the feedback and reports that he needed in a way that everybody could win. The challenge for Bob and all of us is to slow down long enough to look at what we are doing and what we need to learn. His ability to be authentic, humble and genuine with Chuck was excellent. He was also willing to affirm Chuck and his people and co-create solutions.

Bob Cleans it up with Karen and his Management Team

That afternoon Bob met with Karen and spent thirty minutes reconnecting and dealing with his blaming her and being reactive. Bob asked for Karen's input on how she could more effectively manage his schedule. Bob and Karen then looked at creating an ideal weekly schedule and monthly schedule and his key performance objectives for the next two months.

As they were closing he shared with her, "I really need your support. You have been with the company over eight years, I really appreciate your keeping calm in the midst of my being dictatorial and critical. You take good care of me and and do a great job organizing our administrative projects and coordinating my schedule. I will do my best to follow the schedule and not fill it too full of appointments and meetings. Thanks for your support. I like your suggestion that I be accountable to you, that we touch base at least once a day to coordinate my priorities, needs, and any major changes. I really appreciate your contribution and support."

Stepping into a bird's eye view perspective . . . Bob was able to effectively look at the four steps in the coaching process and rebuild his connections and relationship with Karen.

1. Build rapport and play in her world, understanding her feelings and frustration at the absence of authority to fulfill her responsibility

2. Discover and hear her needs and concerns

3. Do performance coaching and training to set up new systems and ideas.

4. They co-created and set up a clear action plan on how to move forward so that his schedule was managed effectively and she derived satisfaction from her contribution to the cause so they could both win.

Bob, like all of us, needs to work on slowing down enough to really be with and affirm the people that he works with that he truly appreciates. It's too easy to get focused on our short-term results, rather than partner with the people that we work with day-to-day to achieve those results through relatedness.

Summary of Key Ideas

In the new millennium we are moving from an old hierarchical paradigm to a new partnering paradigm of shared responsibility and decision-making. In the new paradigm, we are liberated to involve and capitalize on the potential of every employee. We are freeing people to co-create vision, goals, new products and new services that truly serve the needs of contemporary society. Everyone wants to experience genuine communication and mutual respect. Through partnership coaching we are able to help each other achieve our intended results, have our ideas heard and respected and solve the key problems that are before us.

The new paradigm and way of relating is characterized by partnering and teamwork. We need new skills and attitudes to function in this new paradigm. We are learning how to co-create results with partners, give and receive support, have two-way communication and release the true potential of all of our employees. We are challenged to achieve top results through relatedness. We need to learn how to be productive and effective and at the same time connected and related.

To be effective in the team building process, we need to understand the four steps in an effective coaching process:

1. Create rapport with other people
2. Discover needs, problems and concerns
3. Do performance coaching as we set up new solutions and strategies
4. Set action plans and create clear accountability and mutual support.

For companies to thrive in the new millennium, their people need to co-create: sharing vision, goals, business systems, and team culture. Partnership coaching is the essential leadership skill needed to co-create these desired outcomes. In partnership coaching, we give and receive feedback, teach, support, and are accountable. To be part of a winning team takes the courage to be coachable and to be open to learning, and growing every day.

Challenge and Call to Action

As you have read this chapter, I hope you can be understanding and compassionate with Bob because he is every man and woman in the new millennium. He is committed to getting excellent results and working with people, yet each day he falls short of the ideal and standard. He, like all of us, is learning the team-building process as he is trying to integrate new skills and these distinctions into his business and his life. We all need to be patient and compassionate with others and ourselves and be willing to be coached and to learn from everyone we work with and live with. Ask yourself, what problem or process would be best improved or be perfected through creating an effective team to work on it? What person in your organization or your life do you need to clarify things with to have a better relationship? What person or persons in your organization do you need to affirm more frequently? How can you create more mutual support with the people that you work with? It takes a lot of courage to be an authentic team leader and a person that is willing to give and receive coaching.

ABOUT TOM GUZZARDO

Tom Guzzardo works with business owners who want to grow their businesses. Through consulting, coaching and development of educational resources, he partners with business owners and entrepreneurs committed to breakthroughs in their businesses and personal lives. Tom and his team, "the Partner Coaches," provide in-depth programs on Partnership Leadership, Quantum Business Growth and Life Balance & Mastery.

Regardless of the size of your firm, Tom Guzzardo gets results. Tom and his senior consultants deliver customized training, seminars and keynote speeches that increase team effectiveness and productivity, which increases profits.

Contact Information:
Tom Guzzardo
Guzzardo Leadership Group
109 Holly Ridge Road
Stockbridge, GA 30281

Phone: (770) 474-1889
Fax: (770) 474-0442
E-mail: E-mail@TomGuzzardo.com
Web: www.TomGuzzardo.com

Wisdom of Winners: Creating Dual Motivation to Get Immediate Results!

by Jennifer Webb

I t was the first of many seminars I would be doing for the Navy, and this particular morning there was a very distinguished looking man near the front row wearing so many medals he would have immediately set off alarms at any airport security. He was austere and imposing, sitting slightly forward in his chair with a rather stern expression on his face. By the morning break I was beginning to think there was a real problem. He looked uncomfortable, not pleased to be where he was. During the break too much was happening for me to talk with him, and during the second half of the morning he didn't look any less formidable. So you can imagine my surprise when he came sauntering up to me at lunch and asked if we could speak for a minute. Here it comes, I thought, wondering what I was in store for with this man.

"Are there any books you could recommend," he quietly asked. "I'm getting so much from your seminar, but I can't stay for the afternoon, and I have very low self-esteem."

Had there been a feather anywhere close by it would have easily knocked me over. All the rank and accomplishments meant nothing to him because he apparently could not draw upon his own self-worth. People learn from being led, not told, and my hunch is he would have had a lot of trouble getting others to give him the real respect he was due, since he didn't believe in himself.

So what makes us capable of achieving and accomplishing whatever we want in life? Why can some of us lead others to achieve greatness or motivate ourselves to overcome amazing adversity and excel, and others, with all the advantages in the universe, still can't succeed? Exactly what is it that we need to do in order to motivate ourselves and others to reach past our potential? What do we need to know, and how can we find out? Until we can understand how to draw this out in ourselves and others, we will not be able to maximize our teams to their full potential.

General George S. Patton said, "Never tell people how to do things. Tell them what you want them to achieve and they will surprise you with their ingenuity."

So what do we need to know to motivate others to surpass their own limits and expectations, and how can we apply this formula first and foremost to our own lives professionally and personally?

It's been said 90 percent of initial communication is nonverbal. So it stands to reason that people pick up on our nonverbals — our tone, body language, conviction, and self-confidence — before they react to the content of what we're saying. In his book, *Working with Emotional Intelligence*, Daniel Goleman states that 25 percent of our success comes from IQ, 75 percent from how we deal with ourselves and others emotionally (hence, emotional intelligence, EQ). What's my point? We communicate what we feel and believe much more loudly and clearly than the words we're speaking. (Poet Ralph Waldo Emerson said, "What you are shouts so loudly that I cannot hear what you say.") And if there's an incongruity in what we're saying and what we're projecting, people sense we aren't what we appear to be.

So in order to create a winning team environment, and to have what you want in life, whether you are part of a start-up company, selling stocks or working for yourself, it's essential to re-examine your current beliefs — decide what needs changing and take steps to create new beliefs that will get you the results you want now.

We communicate our beliefs in everything we say and do. The exercise at the end of this chapter is part of a formula I've shared with thousands of people over the years to create exactly what they want in life. It is an effective tool. It works!

Several years ago I remember getting an assignment from *The New York Times* to write a travel article, and at the time I mentioned this assignment to a woman I knew who immediately responded, "Man, you were born under a lucky star." She called me a "golden child," meaning someone who things came to easily, when in fact the "gold" came from the hours I spent each evening sending query letters to publications. This, of course, was something she didn't see.

Actually, of all the things I might have been born under, a lucky star wasn't one of them. In fact, the reason I earn a living today sharing insights with audiences around the world on creating smarter results is because I was such an expert years ago at not getting what I wanted. I would venture to say I knew more about failure and not succeeding than most.

When I was ten, my mother died, my dad had a breakdown after her death, and I raised myself. I met a cute guy when I was thirteen years old, dated this guy until I was seventeen, at which time I married him. I had a couple of children, got left by the cute guy for another woman, got evicted from my home because I ran out of money, got cancer . . . in other words, life could have been better. While I was wondering why life wasn't exactly going according to my plans, most people were busy telling me that life wasn't fair and one had to take what was dished out, make the best of it, and all sorts of other well-meaning (but highly depressing) platitudes. About this time I was given a book by a friend. It was actually too convoluted for me to get through, but one line just jumped out at me from the page: We create our own reality!

No way, I thought; what a crock! I wouldn't be dumb enough to create this kind of misery for myself. I would have created a nice little home in Hawaii with a great deal of money.

So I closed the book and wasted another ten years or so. Then one day I had an epiphany. I finally got a wake up call that made me realize so much of what had been happening to me I was bringing on myself. And if even part of what happens to us we bring on ourselves, or is the result of how we respond to what is happening, look at the incredible power we have to create change. This ability to "see" conflicts or challenges in a different perspective is essential in bringing resolution to issues within a team structure.

One of the first things we need to do is to quiet the "experts," the people who tell us why something isn't possible and why we must settle or why a project will never work. (By the way, according to the Tuckman Team Building Model, 80 percent of people we work with are easygoing and willing to pull their own share. [Transmitters], 10 percent always see the glass half full and are eager to move forward, [Transformers] and 10 percent are those negative individuals who always throw cold water on projects [Terrorists]. They, unfortunately, contaminate the other 90 percent.) So who needs terrorists? The point is, they don't come to us as terrorists; they come to us as well-meaning colleagues, the morning news, a spouse, good friend or even an echo of voices from our past that define many of the self images we carry around about ourselves. Needless to say I don't believe in experts. Don't get me wrong, I have great respect for people with excellent information within a specific field. It's just that they can't be relied upon to form our conscious beliefs about what we can and can't do. Let me tell you when I stopped believing in experts. When my son, Michael, was a baby he had slight brain damage due to a high fever. He was dyslexic, and since he also had trouble balancing, hearing, speaking clearly, seeing clearly (he had double vision) and assorted other physical problems, I took him to an "expert" in Long Island, New York. After a battery of tests, this neurologist took me aside and told me, in confidence, to send Michael to a nice vocational school because he didn't have the ability to go to college.

I was crushed; I had envisioned Michael in graduate school, which I thought would enable him to do anything he wanted with his life. (Can you imagine being told your child doesn't have the ability to attend college?) I never imagined he wouldn't be able to go to college. So I waited and waited as long as I could before I broke the news to him. In fact, I waited until he had his masters degree in forensic science (and he got a 4.0 grade average) to tell him what the "expert" had said. My point is simple; experts know their stuff, but they don't know you and your abilities, or the abilities and skill-sets of your team, their determination, drive, energy, perseverance, etc. Thank goodness I decided early on to stop letting others make the final decisions about important issues in my life. We should listen, of course, but professionally and personally we need to consider "expert" advice as only one source of information, part of the criteria to be considered.

My first career was in journalism where I interviewed some very interesting people including Orson Welles, Muhammad Ali and Ted Kennedy among others. The second career included different jobs, and ultimately I found myself in a career that wasn't right for me, wasn't where I felt gratified and satisfied — a place I didn't want to stay. I wanted to start my own business; I thought I had something to teach and share. At the time, however, a close friend warned me that if I gave up the security, benefits and comfortable salary of my current job, it would be the biggest mistake of my life.

Don't you just love it when experts are wrong? Fifteen years later the biggest mistake has turned out to be the best move I've ever made, but if I had listened to this friend, who knows where I would have ended up. I've spoken in 44 out of 50 states as well as several countries, and some of the best rewards are when I know I've reached people and given them tools they can immediately put to use. Even better is when they tell me immediately that I've given them something tangible, like the time 650 college kids stood up and gave me a standing ovation. I knew instantly I was exactly where I needed to be.

So let me ask you a trick question here (and before you answer, remember I said trick question); have you ever had a bad day? Now you're possibly thinking that's the craziest question you've ever heard and plan to put the book down right now, but hear me out, even if you feel you've had enough bad days in the past week to fill a yearly calendar. I don't believe you can have a bad day. I think you can have a dreadful morning, a terrible meeting, an awful commute, or a series of bad occurrences, but they constitute a bad day only if you choose to drag them throughout the day, allowing them to gather momentum and speed along the way. We have bad days only if we choose to mentally carry the events that have accumulated (the major client who went South, the credit that was turned down, two hours in a traffic jam due to construction, the busted radiator) throughout the day.

Things happen. We get disappointed, hurt, disillusioned and experience many other frustrations that cause us to feel less than thrilled, yet we still have choices in what we do with our emotion, how we handle the situation. Tell this to most people and the reaction will be something akin to telling them you've suddenly learned to levitate over your desk for relaxation. People so often choose not to believe they have this kind of control because it means they must take responsibility, and can no longer blame circumstances, a boss, politics or anything else for not being where they want to be. It's easier to say things like "he just ruined my day," or "she always makes me so mad." Nonsense, things happen. But if we choose to carry that negative energy throughout the day, then we can certainly get extra momentum and probably not have to worry about solving an issue; we're too busy being angry or slighted or right-eously upset. A good motto to remember, when you have no control and can't do anything about the situation, is F.I.D.O. (forget it, and drive on).

Viktor Frankl, a Jewish psychiatrist in a German concentration camp, noted in his book, *Man's Search for Meaning,* that fellow inmates at the camp actually chose whether or not they lived or died; not whether they were thrown in the ovens, but whether they chose to live. He used the example of someone who thought "what's the use?" and just gave up, quit trying. This individual would quietly die. Others, he noted, kept focusing on getting back to find out if their wives had survived or to be reunited with their children, and they lived. The major difference — their attitudes. And this is one of the major differences between mediocrity and greatness, how we leverage our attitude and the attitudes of others to use as a catalyst to get team "buy in," to get people really involved. By the way, one sad example Frankl shared in his book was of a man who dreamed of rescue, dreamed of freedom, and in his dream saw a specific date. Nearer and nearer to that date he became more vibrant and ener-getic, and when the day came and passed with no rescue, he inexplicably became weaker and weaker until he died, days before their release.

We have the power to control our attitude, and this power has everything to do with how we motivate ourselves, how we influence others, and how effectively and brilliantly we live our lives. Of course we've all heard the adage that life is 10 percent what happens to us and

90 percent what we do about it. Now think a second; if we begin to understand and use techniques to channel and control this power, we have tremendous options available.

If we think about the power of thought, it's good to explore Dr. Karen Shanor's book *The Emerging Mind* with contributions from several leading experts, including Dr. Deepak Chopra. Dr. Shanor reminds us that the old saying, "Be careful what you ask for, you might get it" might be expanded upon to include the warning "Be careful what you think of, it just might happen." She asserts that some scientists believe our thoughts are capable of creating matter. Pretty exciting stuff. The point is, we have incredible power, so what are some ways we can really begin to make use of it, how can we get smarter faster and shorten our learning curve to utilize this information to the fullest?

Let's begin by assuming we can change how we've been thinking and how we've been doing things in order to get the specific results we want. And let's also assume that there are people out there right now who understand this principle and are utilizing it to motivate teams, close more deals, live a happier life, do the work they enjoy or whatever is important to them. In other words, if someone else has already figured out how to create different behavior and results by changing beliefs, then we can most assuredly do the same.

Before you continue reading, take a second and imagine you're sitting in one of my seminars and I hold up a sign and ask you to glance at it for two seconds and then to read it back to me. You look at it and respond, "The Birds Sing in the Spring." Common mistake, because the sign really reads "The Birds Sing in the the Spring." However, when our brain rapidly scans the words, it edits out the second "the." That's what we do every day, size up a situation immediately based on old criteria, old beliefs, all that old information. Can you see how easy it is to get stuck in the kind of thinking that limits us from ever moving forward?

So if the premise here is that we have control over what we're thinking, and what we're thinking either limits us and drags us down or allows us to move forward, keeps us from becoming stuck and enables us to see alternative solutions to situations, then our job is to figure out how to harness and control our thoughts.

Take a minute right now and do the following. First, decide on one goal (this exercise is listed at the end of the chapter) that is really important to you — making vice president, increasing your salary by 20 percent, buying a larger house, whatever — and be very specific and willing to do whatever it takes to make it happen. If the goal was to increase your salary by 20 percent, why didn't you write down 45 percent, and if the idea is ludicrous to you, then why? Aren't you worth it? Re-examine why you don't feel you're worth that kind of salary increase. Let's begin by creating a relatively high goal (people tend to set low expectations so as not to be disappointed, and guess what, they never are). What we focus on expands, and, consequently, if we spend the day worrying about paying bills and feeling annoyed that someone who does half the work makes twice the money we do, guess what we'll continue to get . . . more work with less financial remunerations (that's called self-fulfilling prophecy). What we focus on really does expand.

So back to the exercise. You've thought of one thing that is really worth achieving. Now list reasons why you can't reach your goal and/or the fears that get in the way — fear of failure, of mistakes, of looking foolish, etc. Fear is one of the main reasons we often remain paralyzed instead of taking action. And when we examine these fears, often what we notice is we're bringing along a lot of beliefs that were dumped on us at an early age, beliefs that have nothing to do with our adult lives, but we still can't seem to shake them off. An example might be that you want to start your own business within the next year, but . . . you know there are already so many people doing what you do that your chances would be slim-to-none that you could survive, and don't forget those statistics about how many businesses close down within three years, and remember in college how several professors said you were smart but had a short attention span and lacked follow-through. If we believe what we're told, we're often subjected to other people's disappointments. Stands to reason if I wanted to start my own business but was too afraid, then why in the world would I want you to succeed; it would simply point out my inadequacies. And the scary thing is, I might not even realize I was throwing cold water on your dream. It would be a reflexive, knee-jerk kind of reaction.

If we listen to others, we might as well not bother trying. I mentioned the "expert" who warned me my son would never go to college, the friend who said starting my own business would be the biggest mistake of my life, and the list really is endless. If we stop to think about it, we've all got these lists. So just how badly do you want something? Talk is cheap. We've got to be willing to do whatever is necessary in order to get the results we want.

When my son was a teenager, he decided one day that he wanted to meet the actress Brooke Shields. I ignored him on this, but somehow he found Brooke's lawyer's address and started sending poetry to the lawyer's office. When that didn't work, Michael began taking the number seven train from Queens, New York, where we lived at the time, into Manhattan where he hand delivered single flowers to the office.

Now this got the lawyer's attention; Michael was being a pest. So he was turned over to Brooke's agent, her aunt. After a year or so of conversation we get a call one day. Brooke was shooting a scene from a movie, "Endless Love," and she would wait for us. Michael got to be photographed with her; she hugged him, talked with him, and when we got back home, I found him sitting on his bed writing all over his tube socks with a green magic marker. When I asked him what in the world he was doing, he responded that he wanted to remember those were the socks he was wearing the day he met Brooke Shields. He did something seemingly impossible because he wasn't willing to give up, and he was willing to do whatever it took.

When I started my business I announced to everyone that I was going in the speaking and training business. I had no clients, no referrals, and very little money. I made about fifty calls a day, couldn't pay rent some months, and often felt like giving up, but not enough to quit. The first major client I landed was Chemical Bank. I was hired by the head of their Human Resource department to deliver two, half-day seminars, and when we had lunch prior to the training, I asked her what prompted her to hire me (of course I was fishing for a compliment). She looked me straight in the eye and said, "You just kept calling."

So you decide on something, you've listed all the excuses you could use to shut yourself down, and you've created a plan comprised of small steps that are dated. This way you will have a series of SOS's (series of small successes) as you move forward. It's important to recognize each small step forward; it's a cumulative process.

And be aware, if your goal is not something within the corporate arena, (where you would automatically communicate and share information with staff or team members) you must still make sure people know of your plans. Otherwise, it's too easy to fall back and not follow through.

And what happens if you fail, or make a big mistake that knocks you on your backside? Exactly what all the millionaires and successful people before you have done: pick up and start over. In fact you should congratulate yourself if this happens because you're a survivor, and in the ranks of fine company. Don't forget Walt Disney was fired for not being creative, and legendary dancer/actor Fred Astaire had a framed rejection memo that read (and I'm paraphrasing) "He can't sing, can't act, can dance a little."

Back to the exercise. Look to see who is already doing what you plan to accomplish, then see how you can tap into their knowledge base. Next, use all your learning styles/intelligences. It's been proven that when you use a at least two modalities at the same time (hear and read something simultaneously, move about [kinesthetic] and look at something [visual]) you speed up the process of learning, creating and retaining information. And one great way to ensure success is to make your goals visual. Use imagery, use a photo, find a way to visualize what you want. Stephen Covey, in *Seven Habits of Highly Successful People,* told people to begin with the end in mind. "See it as if you've already got it." Good advice. One Heisman trophy winner actually put a photo of all the events he was going to win on the ceiling above his bed . . . first thing he looked at in the morning and last thing he saw before he fell asleep.

Watch what you're thinking and monitor your negative thoughts (it's been said we are constantly having a dialogue with ourselves, going at the speed of 600 to 800 words per minute, and most of the time we don't want to hear what we're saying). This is very true within a team environment where one negative comment can deplete morale and erode productivity. Write down negative thoughts you hear yourself saying each day, keeping in mind it's the awareness of what you're thinking and the repetition of changing negative thought patterns that creates positive results! Negative thought example: "Yeh, I'm going to try what she said, but I've read this kind of information before; it won't really work for me. And anyway, I'm at the conference all next week and really don't have any spare time, so I won't do the exercises." Next, be sure to create a game plan to respond to all those "voices," those people who will remind you something will inevitably go wrong, that you can't make it happen.

Author Richard Bach, who wrote a clever little book in the 60's called *Jonathan Livingston Seagull* said, "Argue for your limitations and you get to keep them." By the way, his book was turned down by fifty-one publishers, and a few years ago JLS was in print more than any other publication except *Webster's Dictionary* and the *Bible*. So Bach knew a thing or two about monitoring his thoughts and follow-through.

Don't forget, as you create change and growth and continue to move forward, it probably won't feel all that great, and it could feel downright uncomfortable. That's what change is all about, and that's where most people drop change like a hot potato. Keep in mind this is where it is up to you to educate team members that the process of change will feel uncomfortable, but the end results will be worth the discomfort. Take a second right now and quickly write your signature. Good, now put your pen in your non-dominant hand and write your signature again.

Feels awkward, right? So does growth. But it's imperative to keep going. The alternative is to stay exactly where you are, and that's when we begin to settle. Life is too short to wake up with regrets, especially when there are so many choices and opportunities available to you to have what you want, to reach and surpass your goals. Will Rogers said, "Even if you're on the right track, you'll get run over if you just sit there." Remember if we continue to "sit there" we're certainly going to be safe, but "there" is where we'll stay. If our teams "sit there" without embracing change, they will be left behind.

Creating what you want for yourself and your team involves risk, commitment and flexibility. It's an exciting proposition — a paradigm shift — to understand you have the power to choose how you view any situation and, consequently, create personal and professional outcomes based on restructuring beliefs.

This formula works, and continues to work for those willing to use it. It allows us to motivate others to reach their potential, enables us to lead more effectively and helps us shorten our learning curve to create smarter results. Our success depends on our willingness to take action. And now happens to be a wonderful time to begin moving forward!

11-Step Exercise:

1. Decide what you want; be very specific
2. Ask yourself what fears are getting in the way, limiting your growth
3. List all the excuses you could use
4. Write a plan, utilizing the small steps to celebrate the SOS's
5. Tell people; announce your goal
6. Find people who are already achieving this goal; shorten your learning curve
7. Use all your intelligences, all your learning styles
8. Look at your goal from different perspectives, i.e. look at other industries, alternative sources for inspiration, creative tools like Roger vonOech's "Creative Whack Pack" and Edward de Bono's methodologies
9. Start NOW, not tomorrow. Do one step today, or put this away until you're really serious about your goal
10. Create a game plan for anyone who tells you you can't accomplish your goal
11. Monitor your progress. Be aware of just how much you've accomplished to be where you are in your life personally and professionally right now. Be proud of your progress, keep focused on your objective, and have fun in the process!

ABOUT JENNIFER WEBB

Jennifer Webb, President of Magic Communications, L.L.C., has educated, motivated, empowered and entertained people in 45 states, Europe and South America, using the visual imagery of magic and clever "left brain" and "right brain" tools designed to accelerate adult learning. She has taught thousands how to transform their lives by refocusing their thoughts to change their beliefs, which changes their actions. Her former work as a journalist provides her a solid foundation for researching and creating training materials. Jennifer's diverse client list includes Goldman Sachs, Marriott Hotels, Revlon, Volvo, Deloitte & Touche, the U.S. Navy and the U.S. Postal Service.

Jennifer's professional affiliations have included the National Speakers Association, the Society for Human Resource Management, the New York Society for Association Executives, Women in Communications and Meeting Planners International. She is the mother of two and an avid runner. She lives in Manhattan with her cocker spaniel, Shakespeare.

Contact Information:
Jennifer Webb
Magic Communications
85 East End Ave., 3B
New York, NY 10028

Phone: (212) 628-7411
Fax: (212) 628-8209
E-mail: MagicComm@aol.com
Web: www.MagicComm.com

Zap the Gap:
Working with Team Members
from Multiple Generations

by Meagan Johnson

Early in my working career, I was asked to be the team leader of a high-profile sales group. (We were part of a large copier company.) Imagine my excitement as I got to choose my own team! The very first person I chose was Doug, a card-carrying Generation X person. He was part of the generation that was rumored to be difficult to manage, flaky, unreliable, disloyal, and self-centered.

These things did not worry me because I am a Gen X-er myself. With the myopia that can be typical of someone new to a leadership position, I figured that if we were the same age, we could not be so different. Did I choose Doug for his product knowledge? No . . . this was his first job out of college and he knew very little about the copiers we sold. Did I choose Doug for his strong work ethic? No . . . I didn't know him well enough to identify that. Did I choose Doug because customers loved him? Well, we had not made calls together at that point . . . so I really didn't know that either. I did choose Doug for his energy, which he had in spades. He always arrived at work with a smile on his face, and he seemed to learn new things very quickly.

Doug had been on my team a few weeks when something happened that led me to re-evaluate the "connection" I thought we had. I was finishing lunch one day in the sales rep room when Doug came in. As usual, Doug seemed happy and enthusiastic. I asked him how lunch went; he replied in his typically enthusiastic voice that it had been "Grrrreat!" Glad for his happiness, and curious about where I could get some of this "Grrrreat" lunch, I asked him what had made lunch such a wonderful experience.

"Well," he said, "I made $15 at lunch today."

Now I consider myself an inveterate networker, someone who seizes every opportunity to identify potential customers, but I had never made $15.00 at lunch. Besides, in our business, a typical commission would have two or three more zeros after the decimal. So I bit and asked him how he made $15.00 at lunch. His reply was that when he paid the cashier, he paid with a ten-dollar bill but received change for a twenty.

Call me slow, but I asked him how he made money after he told her about the mistake and gave her back the change.

"Give the change back! Now why would I want to do anything like that?" he asked. The first words that came out of my mouth were "Because it is the right thing to do."

"Who says it is the right thing?" asked Doug. "After all, it's her fault, not mine, isn't it?"

I thought about Doug's question. Who did say it was the right thing? While I mulled it over, a memory came back to me.

I was five years old and my dad and I had gone to the grocery store. As the cashier rang up my father's purchase, she misread the price tag and charged my father 69¢, rather than the $1.69 marked on the tag. "No," my father said, "it is not 69¢. It is $1.69."

The cashier thanked my father and rang up the item at the correct price. As we left the store, I asked my father why he had told the cashier about the mistake. "You could have had that dishwashing detergent for only 69¢. You would have saved a dollar!"

At the time, my weekly allowance was a dollar. The idea that my father would willingly spend more when he could have gotten away with spending less seemed crazy. A dollar was a lot of money to me then.

My father's reply was: "My self-worth is worth more than a dollar."

I have carried that memory with me all my life; as a result, it has influenced many ethical decisions I have had to make.

I shared this memory with Doug, thinking it would enlighten him.

His reply was "You have got to be kidding! I did not even know my father. My parents divorced, and he moved away when I was very young. I rarely saw my mother. She worked two jobs to support us. There were two ways to make extra money. One was that you kept extra change and the second was to swipe tips off the tables at restaurants."

I was shocked by Doug's answer. As more Generation X sales reps came back from lunch that day, I asked them how they would handle a similar situation. It was a big surprise to me when everyone agreed with Doug.

With this experience in mind, I began to survey my customers about their experiences with Generation X. When asked to list words to describe my generation, the words and phrases selected included: unreliable, tardy, dressed sloppily, unethical, does not respect older management, not loyal, questions everything, self-centered, and all they want to do is have fun.

Ironically, the same words were used thirty years ago to describe Baby Boomers, those people who are between the ages of thirty-six and sixty-four today. Baby Boomers' managers thought they were lazy, unreliable, tardy, dressed sloppily, unethical, did not respect older management, were not loyal, questioned everything, were self-centered, and all they wanted to do was have fun.

What we are saying about new employees is not new. Managers say the same thing about every new work force. What we are really describing is a youthful generation.

According to the *American Heritage Dictionary*, the definition of "youthful" is: *Possessing youth; still young; in an early stage of development.* Generation X and the generation following, the Echo Generation, are the new players in the work force. They are still young and in an early stage of development. Therefore many of the traits they exhibit can be written off to their lack of development and maturity.

On the other hand, they do bring a new set of experiences and ethics to the teams they join, based on experiences they've had that are unique to their generation.

These different experiences are called signposts. Signposts are the experiences and situations that give our lives a sense of purpose and direction. Signposts influence the decisions we make from day to day. My father's lesson about returning change was a personal signpost in my life.

There are also generational signposts that define an entire generation. The Vietnam War was a generational signpost that helped shape my father's generation. As a Gen X-er, the plethora of single-parent families in the 1970's and 1980's helped shape mine.

Generations in the Workplace Today

There are four generations working side-by-side in the workforce today, each bringing its own generational and personal signposts to the workplace:

Traditionals — born between 1909 and 1945

Baby Boomers — born between 1946 and 1964

Generation X-ers — born between 1965 and 1975

Echo Boomers — born between 1976 and 1986

Traditional Generation

These folks were raised in the Great Depression. They grew up listening to Fred Allen, Amos and Andy, and Fibber McGee and Molly on the radio. The words we often use to describe people of this generation are hardworking, loyal, patient and tenacious.

Traditional Generation Signposts

The events that influenced this generation, including the Great Depression and World War II, taught them the value of persistence and tenacity. The signposts this generation acquired said, "If you hung in there, you would eventually be rewarded." *You learned to follow the rules.* If you didn't, you risked losing your job and your very means of survival.

With hard work and the help of government programs like the WPA and CCC, this generation survived the Great Depression. They went on to defeat Germany, Italy and Japan in WWII, they rebuilt Europe and Japan after the war, they staved off the spread of communism, and they contributed to the creation of the consumer market (washing machines, dryers, dishwashers, microwave ovens and televisions) that we know today.

The GI Bill made education more available for this generation than for any other. In 1947, 50 percent of college students were in school with the help of the GI Bill. These college graduates ultimately earned an average of forty percent more than their peers who did not take advantage of this opportunity.

Housing became affordable. Production building processes (houses built as if they were on an assembly line in huge housing developments) and government insured loans made homes more affordable. The average cost of a home was $7,000, less than most of us spend on a used car today.

The signposts this generation carried away — hard work, follow the rules, be loyal, be patient and be tenacious — influence them still in the workplace today. When we think of this generation, we often think of old people sitting on the porch, watching the world pass them by. Or we think of this generation spending their years in a nursing home, when in reality only 1 percent of this generation needs nursing home care.

The reality is that this generation, more than any other, does not really "retire." Many companies have come to realize the value these folks bring to the workplace and actively recruit them. They come to work on time, they're loyal, they do what they say they will do, they don't flirt with co-workers or customers (the hormones have died down), and they do a good job. Super-retailer Wal-Mart differentiated itself from its competitors by placing an elderly Greeter at the front of each store. In the competitive discount retail market, every bit of differentiation helps.

The Baby Boomers

With fifteen years of deprivation from the Great Depression and World War II behind them, Traditional Generation servicemen came home from the war, married, and started producing babies in record numbers. Between 1946 and 1964, 77 million new Americans were born — creating the largest demographic generation in history. This generation was approximately twice the size of their parent's generation — hence the name "Baby Boomers."

Baby Boomer Signposts

With the economic prosperity following WWII, the Traditionalists worked hard to provide their Baby Boomer children with everything they (the Traditionalists) had never had. A nice home, modern conveniences, and education became the norm. With the exception of scares such as the polio epidemic of the 1950's and the unrealized threat of nuclear war,

(Baby Boomers still remember all those air raid drills at school in the 50's), physical survival was largely taken for granted. Unlike their parents, young Baby Boomers never had to go to bed hungry.

Since most Baby Boomers had all their basic needs given to them throughout their childhood, as they came of age in the 1960's, they had the luxury of exploring issues that were higher on Maslow's hierarchy: the equality of women, civil rights, and rightness or wrongness of American military action in Vietnam. Additionally, they felt free to question the rules and values that their parents accepted as unquestionable.

And much good came from their efforts. The Vietnam War was brought to an end. An unethical president was forced to resign. Women were empowered to enter the work force and receive equal pay for equal work. The Civil Rights Act was passed, marking the beginnings of the erasure of racial discrimination.

But not all was positive. Traditional family structures fell victim to experimentation in alternative life styles. In the wake of all this experimentation, this generation produced the highest divorce rate in history. Consequently, more Generation X-ers (the children of these Baby Boomers) come from broken and single-parent homes than any previous generation.

With the advent of the Pill, the Baby Boomers could postpone having children as a matter of convenience. During the 1960's, concern about world over-population, combined with the relative ease of controlling conception, led to a drastic reduction in the average size of a family. Consequently, the 1970's and 1980's, a time when the Baby Boomers would have normally been producing record numbers of offspring, were instead marked by a drastic decline in the birth rate. Thus, the generation these Baby Boomers created was half the size of their Baby Boomer parents' generation.

Disillusioned Hippies Become Yuppies

By the end of the 1970's, the idealism of the Baby Boomer generation had soured. The world they had envisioned at Woodstock had not come to fruition. They had been raised during the economically prosperous 50's and 60's. Financial security had been the bedrock upon which they could create social change and "do their own thing." Now, events like the end of the Vietnam War and the oil embargo of 1974 had caused a major economic recession. Ultra-high inflation, soaring interest rates and extreme economic uncertainty dominated most of the decade. On the political front, the Watergate scandal, Nixon's resignation and Nixon's pardon by Gerald Ford, dominated the news. These events were followed less than four years later by the Iran Hostage Crisis.

The idealism of the Baby Boomer/Woodstock Generation morphed into cynicism and an attitude that said, "The world is unsavable, so get what you can for yourself as soon as you can." And as the economy rebounded under the Reagan administration, Baby Boomers saw the opportunity to get theirs. From under the Hippies of the 1960's and 1970's crawled the Yuppies of the 1980's.

Implications for Working with Baby Boomers

Since recovering from the recession of the early 90's, Baby Boomers have achieved the kind of financial security they enjoyed as children in the 1950's. They now have time to become nostalgic for the past. We see icons from their youth play prominent parts in advertising Boomer-type products. Janis Joplin pitches for Mercedes Benz, the Rolling Stones for Microsoft, and the Beatles for GTE and Nike. Harley-Davidson motorcycles have staged a roaring come-back among this group. It's as if they are longing for a return to their more rebellious, idealistic youth.

It is not a coincidence that charity contributions from this age group are at an all-time high. Boomers today are looking for a similar commitment from the companies that hire them. They want to know that what they are doing is going to leave a positive impact, not on just the company, but on the community that the boomer lives in and supports.

Target Department Store recognizes this and donates a portion of its proceeds back to the community each year. Xerox selects employees (usually baby boomers) to take a year off with full pay and benefits to work with the charity of the employee's choice. More and more companies are giving their employees family leave days, charity contribution matches, and time off to work with the less fortunate in the community. These efforts keep the Baby Boomers actively involved in their teams with the knowledge that their work is contributing to a greater good.

Generation X

Unlike their Baby Boomer parents, who were born and raised in a time of peace and prosperity, Generation X-ers were born into the tumultuous and unsure world of the 1970's. They watched their parents struggle to find work and make ends meet, and they watched their parents' transition from hippie idealism to yuppie cynicism. They began to collect their generational signposts just as their yuppie parents were creating the decade of consumption. The BMW replaced the VW as the car with cachet. Nutra Sweet promised us victory over sugar. Slogans like "Shop till You Drop" and "He Who Dies with the Most Toys Wins" were often observed on bumper stickers.

To support this attitude toward living and spending, most Baby Boomer households had both parents working. In single-parent households (which was the case for more than half of all households in the United States) that parent often worked two jobs just to keep up. Consequently, Generation X was the first generation to come home from elementary school to an empty house. Long before they acquired the label of Generation X, members of this generation were known as latch key kids.

It is easy to assume that this was a bad thing. Imagine that you were a ten-year-old who had to spend three hours at home alone every day after school. You probably suffered from feelings of loneliness. You were probably bored a lot. And you may have gotten into some mischief (lots of them certainly did). You also learned that the television could be your primary form of entertainment.

Of course, as pre-school children, these Latch Key/Generation X kids had learned to read from Burt and Ernie on *Sesame Street*. They learned their math from Count Dracula. Their table manners came from the Cookie Monster, and Oscar the Grouch taught them social skills. During those hours alone after school, they spent hours playing Nintendo games that could be played solo; they were excited by action cartoons that glorified violence; and they were titillated by soap operas that taught them sexual morals and social values.

Meanwhile, they had grown up with, and taken for granted, microwave ovens, remote control TV's, dishwashers, dryers, and fast food. They learned that if they couldn't have mom or dad's company and attention, they could probably guilt trip them into lavish allowances. As children, Generation X had more spending money than any group before them.

Consequently, expectations of being constantly entertained and instantly gratified became powerful signposts for this generation.

Non-commitment Becomes a Signpost for Generation X

Generation X-ers witnessed their parents dedicate themselves to their employers, often at the expense of their families and then watched those same employers, after the October, 1987 stock market crash, dump their parents in wave after wave of re-engineering, restructuring, and reductions in force. Consequently, the signpost left with many Generation X-ers was: "Don't commit to any company because, in the end, you can count only on yourself."

This signpost has led Generation X-ers to value personal and career development over commitment to a company. The average Gen X-er will stay on the job less than two years, and is expected to change careers eight or more times before retiring. When asked, Gen X-ers often say they do not leave a job because they are dissatisfied with working conditions or pay, but because they feel the job does not mesh with their personal and professional goals.

Implications for Working With Generation X

The challenge for an employer who wants to motivate and retain good Gen X workers, then, is to provide them with not just a job, but with an experience that will contribute to their development. For example, I am a partner with a consulting firm that uses a local printer. The lead graphic artist for this printer is a talented, twenty-seven year-old Gen X-er. She recently informed us that she was leaving to work for another printer. We asked her if it was an increase in salary that had lured her away, and she replied that she was actually taking a cut in pay. We then asked her if it were her working conditions. (Maybe she didn't get along with the owner of the print shop.) "No," she said. She gets along fine with him.

"Why," we asked, "are you leaving then?"

Her reply: "I get to do cooler stuff on the computer there."

It seems to me that if our printer had wanted to hold on to this talented artist, he would have been well served to create the opportunity for her to do "cool stuff" at his shop.

When teams look at the duties and job tasks that members perform, and can identify what the benefit to the Generation X employee is in completing those tasks and duties, the possibility of recruiting and retaining that employee increases.

The Echo Boom Generation

Born between 1976 and 1994, the latest group to enter today's work force is the Echo Boomer Generation. So named because of its sheer numbers (72 million), this generation "echos" the size of the Baby Boom Generation (77 million). Additionally, this generation has not stopped growing and is predicted to reach 82 million by 2001.

The reasons for the enormous size of the Echo Boom are twofold. In the late 80's and mid 90's, Generation X-ers were reaching an age where they were starting to have children. Secondly, during that same period aging Baby Boomers, many of them in their second (or third) marriages, decided it was time to have the children they had postponed during their Woodstock years.

Echo Boomer Signposts

Echo Boomers tend to be better educated than their predecessors. Many were raised in households run by educated Generation X-ers or by aging Baby Boomers who were determined to "get it right." They're used to having their needs met instantly, and they've been exposed to more information and technology than any previous generation.

Most Baby Boomers learned to use a computer at work, where it was a tool to get the job done more quickly and easily. Generation X began using computers in high school or college. The Echo Boomers, on the other hand, learned to use a computer at home as a form of entertainment and education before they reached kindergarten.

The Echo Boomers walked into grade school with a firm grasp on how to surf the net, do electronic research, play games and purchase products on e-bay. In many cases, they were able to teach their teachers a thing or two about optimizing the computer's use.

Is there a downside to this technical prowess?

According to the *Wall Street Journal*, it's not unusual for someone who spends a great deal of time developing computer skills to fail to develop his or her people skills. This means that you can have Echo Boom team members who are the most technically savvy people on the planet but lack the basic people skills required to work successfully on a team. Despite their remarkable computer savvy, they'll need nurturing and guidance to develop the complex communication and people skills that most jobs require.

Implications for Working with Echo Boomers

Successful employers will give echo boomers graduated levels of empowerment. For example, a family fun park we work with hires scores of Echo Boomers to operate the rides, oversee the video games and run the concessions. They have created a graduated set of rules and procedures known as blue rules and red rules. When an employee first joins the team, all rules are red. The red rules are very specific: do not spit in front of a customer; say hello to each guest who approaches your counter. The second set of rules are blue rules. Once you have spent some time on the team and followed the red rules, you get a blue tee shirt, which empowers you to break the blue rules when necessary. The blue rules are judgement calls. For example, if a family is riding a ride and their time is up but nobody is waiting in line, a blue-shirted employee can extend the length of the family's ride.

Bubba Gump Shrimp Company, a restaurant chain, instructs its hosts to ask incoming customers, "How are you?" to start the process of engaging the customer in the restaurant experience. This may seem pretty basic, but remember, lack of inter-personal skills is often the Echo Boomer's greatest flaw.

Conclusion

The work-force today consists of four very different generational groups that have very distinct needs. The wise team leader will recognize the differences in these needs and act accordingly. To assist in that process, here is a summary of those differences and what you can do about them:

Generation	Signposts	Implications	Actions
Traditional	• The Great Depression • WWII • Prosperity of the 50's	Hard working, conservative, perseverant, willing to delay gratification, trust in government & big business	Give them jobs that contribute to the team in a significant way. Let them know that you rely on them and appreciate their being there.
Baby Boomers	• Economic prosperity of the 1950's • Civil unrest of the 1960's • Disillusionment of the 1970's • Materialism of the 1980's	As they now approach retirement, they look nostalgically to the past and want to make a difference socially.	Involve them in work that makes a difference to the community.
Generation X-ers	• Economic insecurity of the 1970's • Television as a teacher & entertainer • Latch key resourcefulness • Instant gratification • Watched parents lose their jobs • Watched parents leave home • Watched new parents come and go	Little sense of commitment to the company. They tend to expect instant gratification. They tend to evaluate the merits of a job on how it can further their careers. They expect jobs to be fun. They expect to work independently and not be micro-managed, even when they may need it.	Transition job descriptions into work experiences. Help the Gen X-er see how each job can further his or her career.
Echo Boomers	• Economic security • More education • Computer/technology driven experiences • Youthful inexperience	Although they excel in the digital world, they often lack people skills and problem-solving skills	Provide graduated experiences and training to develop their soft skills.

ABOUT MEAGAN JOHNSON

Meagan Johnson is a Gen X professional speaker who combines humor with rock-solid content to challenge her audience to think differently and act decisively. Her experience in professional sales with Xerox and Quaker Oats provides her an insider's perspective on what makes business relationships succeed.

A Gen X-er herself, Meagan has researched the best practices of 20+ corporations who employ younger people. Her energetic and engaging delivery of the results of this research, combined with immediately usable tips and tools, empowers managers to better manage younger workers. Plus, she teaches people of all ages how to improve their effectiveness across generational lines. Meagan's diverse client list includes the Bureau of Land Management, Chase Bank Credit Card Services, Harley-Davidson Motor Company and Inc. Magazine.

Contact Information:
Meagan Johnson
The Johnson Training Group
9070 N. 82nd Street
Scottsdale, AZ 85258

Phone: (480) 948-5596
Fax: (480) 948-5744
E-mail: Meagan@JohnsonTrainingGroup.com
Web: www.JohnsonTrainingGroup.com

RESOURCE LISTING

Lisa Bell
Global Connections Speakers Bureau
4631 NW 31st Ave., Suite 166
Fort Lauderdale, FL 33309
℮   (954) 972-5515
Fax: (954) 972-0641
E-mail: GlobalWiz@aol.com
Web: www.GlobalConnections.com

Marie Benoit, Ph.D.
Business Enhancement Institute
9622 Ridge Ave.
Fairfax, VA 22030
℮   (703) 267-5650
Fax: (703) 267-6651
E-mail: MBenoit@erols.com

Mary Bryant
Bryant Enterprises
300 West 55th Street
New York, NY 10019
℮   (212) 262-5004
Fax: (212) 262-5004
E-mail: BryantEnt@aol.com
Web: www.Mary-Bryant.com

Steve Cohn
Absolutely Delightful Dreamers
560 Summer Breeze Court
Alpharetta, GA 30005
℮   (770) 667-3042
Fax: (770) 667-3142
E-mail: ADDreamers@aol.com

Juanita Sanders Cribb
Crystal Communications Corporation
P.O. Box 43027
Atlanta, GA 30336-0027
℮   (770) 469-4247
Fax: (770) 413-9534
E-mail: CCCorp98@aol.com
Web: www.JuanitaCribb.com

Marianne Frederick, MHSA
WorkPlay, Inc.
14 Bridgewood Ave.
Taylors, SC 29687
℮   (864) 268-1541
Fax: (864) 268-1541
E-mail: MFredck@aol.com

Jerry L. Fritz
800 Miller Drive
Oregon, WI 53575
℮   (608) 835-9125
Fax: (608) 262-4617
E-mail: JLF@mi.bus.wisc.edu
Web: www.Wisc.edu/mi

Pamper Garner
Pamper Garner & Associates
P.O. Box 390
Chattanooga, TN 37401
℮   (423) 886-6417
℮   (888) 540-0705 (Toll Free)
Fax: (423) 886-4602
E-mail: PamperG@aol.com
Web: www.pamperbear.com

Cecilia B. Grimes
Etiquette Matters
513 W. Glendale Street
Siler City, NC 27344
℮   (919) 742-3616
Fax: (919) 742-3616
E-mail: EtiquetteMatters@mindspring.com
Web: EtiquetteMatters.com

Tom Guzzardo
Guzzardo Leadership Group
109 Holly Ridge Road
Stockbridge, GA 30281
℮   (770) 474-1889
Fax: (770) 474-0442
E-mail: E-mail@TomGuzzardo.com
Web: www.TomGuzzardo.com

RESOURCE LISTING

Val Jennings
Key Concepts, Inc.
P.O. Box 934911
Margate, FL 33093-4911
℃   (954) 970-0922
Fax: (954) 979-2551
E-mail: Vjennings@Key-Concepts.com
Web: www.Key-Concepts.com

Meagan Johnson
The Johnson Training Group
9070 N. 82nd Street
Scottsdale, AZ 85258
℃   (480) 948-5596
Fax: (480) 948-5744
E-mail: Meagan@JohnsonTrainingGroup. com
Web: www.JohnsonTrainingGroup.com

Mike Marino, Jr.
In Person
P.O. Box 9015
Metairie, LA 70055
℃   (504) 833-4405
E-mail: InPerson@gs.net
Web: www.tfrick.com/Marino

Phyllis May, Ph.D.
P.O. Box 2372
Key West, FL 33045
℃   (305) 295-7501
℃   (877) 312-1800 (Toll free)
Fax: (305) 294-7095
E-mail: PmayKeys@mm0.net

Jane Hight McMurry, M.A.
The Etiquette Advantage
P.O. Box 4544
Wilmington, NC 28406
℃   (910) 762-0703
℃   (800) 782-2443-12 (Toll free)
Fax: (910) 762-0703
E-mail: EtqAd@aol.com
Web: IntBusCom@aol.com

Renée Merchant
DELTA SYSTEMS
5621 Somerset Drive
Brooklyn, MI 49230
℃   (517) 592-5463
Fax: (517) 592-5463
E-mail: Renee@4DeltaSystems.com
Web: www.4DeltaSystems.com

Sandy Pointer, M.S.W., LCSW
P.A.C.E.
3695 Cascade Road
Box 172
Atlanta, GA 30031
℃   (404) 349-0221
Fax: (404) 349-8602
E-mail: SandysPointers@cs.com

Renee P. Walkup
SalesPEAK, Inc.
1896 Winchester Trail
Atlanta, GA 30341
℃   (770) 220-0832
Fax: (770) 220-0833
E-mail: Walkup@SalesPEAK.com
Web: www.SalesPEAK.com

Jennifer Webb
Magic Communications
85 East End Ave., 3B
New York, NY 10028
℃   (212) 628-7411
Fax: (212) 628-8209
E-mail: MagicComm@aol.com
Web: www.MagicComm.com

Patti Wood, M.A., CSP
Communication Dynamics
2343 Hunting Valley Drive
Decatur, GA 30033
℃   (404) 315-7397
Fax: (404) 315-9255
E-mail: PattiWood@mindspring.com
Web: www.PattiWood.net